The Failure of Creationism

The Theory That Never Was

Rosa Rubicondior

The Failure of Creationism

Cover images AI generated by ChatGPT4o

The Failure of Creationism

When you show the world you know you need to lie for your faith, you show the world you know your faith is for fools who believe in falsehoods.

Third Party Copyright.

Third party copyright is acknowledged for work not currently in the public domain, reproduced here for criticism and analysis under intellectual rights fair use regulations.

In the opinion of the author, the minimum necessary for effective criticism and analysis whilst retaining the original context, has been reproduced in this work.

ISBN: 979-8300579050

© 2024 Rosa Rubicondior.
All rights reserved.

The Failure of Creationism

Mr Rothchild: (for the plaintiff) (Quoting from *Darwin's Black Box*) "If a theory claims to be able to explain some phenomenon but does not generate even an attempt at an explanation, then it should be banished. Despite comparing sequences and mathematical modeling, molecular evolution has never addressed the question of how complex structures came to be. In effect, the theory of Darwinian molecular evolution, has not published, and so it should perish.

Mr Rothschild. That was your view in 1996?

Michael J. Behe (for the defendants). Yes, that's correct... The detail is actually simply this, that by these publications, I mean detailed rigorous accounts for complex molecular machines, not just either hypothetical accounts or sequence comparisons or such things.

Mr Rothschild: ..., in fact, there are no peer reviewed articles by anyone advocating for intelligent design supported by pertinent experiments or calculations which provide detailed rigorous accounts of how intelligent design of any biological system occurred, is that correct?

Michael J. Behe: That is correct, yes.

> Kitzmiller Vs Dover Area School District Trial transcript: Day 12 (October 19), AM Session, Part 1

Is intelligent design a scientific alternative to contemporary evolutionary theory? No. Intelligent design proponents may use the language of science, but they do not use its methodology. They have yet to propose meaningful tests for their claims, there are no reports of current research on these hypotheses at relevant scientific society meetings, and there is no body of research on these hypotheses published in relevant scientific journals. So, intelligent design has not been demonstrated to be a scientific theory.

> American Association for the Advancement of Science

Contents

Introduction 5
The Evidence from Science 13
    Case 1. New Information by Gene Duplication 15
    Case 2. Marine Snails Observed Evolving 21
    Case 3. Make Do and Mend 24
    Case 4. Doing the Same Thing in Two Different Ways. 29
    Case 5. New Genetic Information Arising Naturally 31
        Horizontal Gene Transfer 38
    Case 6 Evidence of Common Ancestry 43
    Case 7. 'Macro-Evolution' in Just 36 Years 47
    Case 8. 'Non-Existent' Transitional Fossils 55
    Case 9. Closing in on Abiogenesis 68
        Origin of the Genetic Code 84
The Evidence from History 89
    Case 1. Humans Using Fire in Tasmania 89
    Case 2. Change In Earth's Climate 91
    Case 3. Grand Canyon at Rock Bottom 93
    Case 4. The Origin of Domestic Cattle 98
    Case 5. Archaic Hominins Butchering Elephants 100
    Case 6. Humans Spread Across Europe 102
    Case 7. Co-Evolution of Humans and Sled Dogs 104
    Case 8. Two of Our Elephants Are Missing 105
    Case 9. The Neanderthals of the Pyrenees 107
    Case 10. Mass Migration of Farmers into Iberia 111

Case 11. The Mass Extinction that Killed the Dinosaurs 113
Case 11. How The Milky Way Was Formed. 115
Conclusion..121
Appendix I..125
  The Predicted Demise of Evolutionary Biology 125
    1800's Before Darwin's TOE 126
    1800's Post Darwin's TOE 129
    1900s. 131
    1910s 132
    1920s 134
    1930s 136
    1940 137
    1960s 137
    1970s 139
    1980s 140
    1990s (Pre-Wedge)..143
    1990s (Post-Wedge) 149
    2000s 151
    2019 158
    2024 159
Appendix II 161
  Scientists Reject Intelligent Design Creationism 161
    United States 161
      Federal 161
      State and universities..175
    Other countries and international bodies......................178

Contents

Appendix III 189
   The Discovery Institute's Wedge Strategy 189
   INTRODUCTION 189
   THE WEDGE STRATEGY 191
      Phase I. 191
      Phase II. 191
      Phase III. 191
   THE WEDGE PROJECTS 191
      Phase I. Scientific Research, Writing & Publication ... 191
      Phase II. Publicity & Opinion-making 192
      Phase III. Cultural Confrontation & Renewal 192
   FIVE YEAR STRATEGIC PLAN SUMMARY 192
      Phase I 193
      Phase II. 194
   GOALS 195
      Governing Goals 195
      Five Year Goals 195
      Twenty Year Goals 195
      Five Year Objectives 196
   ACTIVITIES 197
References 199
Index 223
Other Books by Rosa Rubicondior 239

The Failure of Creationism

Introduction

A 2015 Pew Research Survey of American adult opinions (1) reported that 65% believed humans and other animals had evolved over times, while 35% believe God had created everything in its present form.

Of those who believe humans have evolved, 35% believed the process was entirely natural, such as by natural selection, while 24% believe God had guided it (5% undecided)[1]

However, when asked what they thought scientists believed, 66% thought scientists agreed that humans had evolved while 29% thought scientists disagreed.

Similarly with regard to the Big Bang, only 42% thought scientists agreed with the Big Bang theory to account for the Universe while a majority (52%) thought scientists were divided on the issue.

These American public perceptions about what scientists believe contrasts markedly with what scientists actually believe. A 2009 Pew Research Survey (2) found that 97% of scientists believe humans had evolved and only 8% of those believed God had played any part in the process. When restricted to scientists associated with the American Association for the Advancement of Science, the figure rose to 98% - i.e., almost total unanimity and probably as near unanimity as you will find in any branch of science.

For biomedical scientists there is no controversy, and any debate is only ever about the precise mechanism, not the general principle, for example, which environmental factors are the main selectors or how much of it was due to genetic drift, etc.

---

[1] Figures do not total 100% due to rounding to the nearest whole numbers

The Failure of Creationism

From these figures of scientific consensus, it is clear that a major plank of the Discovery Institute's 'Wedge Strategy' (3) – to win scientific support for Intelligent Design as an alternative scientific explanation for biodiversity, has been a monumental failure with scientific consensus unchanged since the Wedge Strategy was launched as a five-year plan to win the support of mainstream science, or at least to win over to their cause, some highly influential figures in science, especially the biological sciences.

The Discovery Institute's Wedge Strategy can be found in Appendix III, and the claims and behaviour of the leading figures in creationism, especially in Intelligent Design Creationism should be seen in the light of the aims and objectives of that organization and its adopted strategy for attaining them.

Although they have failed to make any significant inroads into scientific opinion, what has had some limited success, is their campaign to misinform and mislead American public opinion about what the scientific evidence is and what it demonstrates. The American public have been systematically misled into believing there is good scientific evidence to support creationism, and naturally they assume real scientists are aware of these 'difficulties' for the Theory of Evolution and other creationists hobby horses such as the Big Bang and abiogenesis.

To that extent, the Wedge Strategy has succeeded in driving a wedge between the non-scientific public and professional scientists, the vast majority of who accept the Theory of Evolution by descent with modification from a common ancestor as established beyond reasonable doubt – as near as science ever gets to 'proven'.

The Wedge can claim one more major success; not one of which it can be proud, but one which is true and thoroughly deserved, nonetheless. It has shown the scientific and

Introduction

educated world the intellectual bankruptcy and hypocrisy of a fundamentalist religious cult that purports to worship a god of truth, honesty and integrity who told them bearing false witness is a cardinal sin.

Despite being overwhelmingly rejected by the scientific community, creationism, in the guise of intelligent design, staggers on, constantly claiming that the Theory of Evolution is a theory in crisis, despite the continuing dependence of biomedical science on the theory to explain the observed facts and to predict the outcomes of biological experiments and investigations.

Michael J. Behe's[2] grudging admission in the Kitzmiller vs. Dover case that there are no peer reviewed articles by anyone advocating for intelligent design supported by pertinent experiments or calculations which provide detailed rigorous accounts of how intelligent design of any biological system occurred, continues to be true while the scientific community continually provides peer-reviewed evidence for evolution and quite incidentally refutes creationism and confirms the TOE, simply by revealing the facts.

Of course, serious biomedical scientists no longer concern themselves with demonstrating the truth of the Theory of Evolution, which is taken for granted as the unifying theory of biomedical science, and nor do they concern themselves with demonstrating the falsehood of creationism. That is a simple function of the facts as revealed by science.

That the facts are sufficiently explained by the TOE is reason enough not to do what creationists do, and insert their

---

[2] Michael Joseph Behe (born January 18, 1952) is an American biochemist and an advocate of the pseudoscientific principle of intelligent design (ID). Behe serves as professor of biochemistry at Lehigh University in Bethlehem, Pennsylvania, and as a senior fellow of the Discovery Institute's Center for Science and Culture. (Wikipedia)

particular god in the explanation, is enough to falsify the hypothesis (it's no more than that) that a supernatural deity is needed to explain them, and this is the daily conclusion of science. Indeed, how can it be otherwise when science is the investigation of what can be seen, and creationism's god is never present?

Creationists have been predicting the collapse of 'Darwinism' and before Darwin, the collapse of 'uniformitarianism' and other 'materialist' explanations for natural phenomena, since science began to threaten their cherished mythologies and simplistic, magical answers.(see the long list of such claims in Appendix I)

These hopeful claims of the impending collapse of naturalistic explanations for the world about us were given new legs by the creative inventions of Michael J. Behe's and William A. Dembski's[3] invention of the notions of 'irreducible complexity', 'specified complexity' and 'intelligent design', which dressed creationism in a lab coat and made it look like there was good scientific support for Judeo-Christian fundamentalism.

The problems those notions face, unlike genuine science, is that they can never specify an objective test by which they can be validates, so they never rise above the god of the gaps and false dichotomy fallacies, and nor do they provide a basis for predictions (that can be tested and falsified) for biological experiments.

To explain antibiotic resistance or the frequent origins of new strains of viruses, or indeed the origins of new viruses such as

---

[3] William Albert Dembski (born July 18, 1960) is an American mathematician, philosopher and theologian. He was a proponent of intelligent design (ID) pseudoscience, specifically the concept of specified complexity, and was a senior fellow of the Discovery Institute's Center for Science and Culture (CSC).(Wikipedia)

Introduction

the SARS-CoV-2 virus that caused the COVID-19 pandemic, for example, as the work of an unproven deity, acting in some unspecified manner, provides nothing useful by way of a means to combat it.

This lack of a scientific basis for creationism and its uselessness as a scientific tool, is often cites by the very many scientific bodies that oppose its teaching in science classes. That the creationist lobby wish to teach children an idea which has no practical application speaks to the hidden agenda – the imposition of religious dogma by the sneak tactic of dressing it up as science in order to mislead and confuse vulnerable minds. A long list of academic bodies and professional associations, especially those concerned with biomedical fields of science and science education, which have publicly voiced their opposition to the teaching of creationism in any of its guises, together with their reasons for doing so is in Appendix II.

The fact that several witnesses in the Kitzmiller vs Dover case lied under oath about their association with Christian fundamentalist groups (4) (5), with the clear intention of misleading the court over the religious agenda behind teaching creationism in their schools, testified to that agenda and the deceptive tactics by which children were to be misled to achieve it.

Of course, theologians have tried to associate contrary views with evil and hidden agenda and ascribe nefarious motives to those who simply reveal the truth.

Trading on the paranoias that drive conspiracy theories, the claim is often made that it is all a conspiracy to turn people from their god and so undermine their power base and the excuses they have traditionally used to control the lives of others in their own narrow interests.

But is a religion which is so threatened by the truth of the world around them, worthy of consideration as a valid alternative view of reality?

It's a truism that those who lie about science are not showing us they think science is wrong; they are showing us they know science is right, but they have an agenda which requires people to believe otherwise. What possible honourable motive could there be for trying to deceive someone into believing something you know to be false?

That agenda can be seen in the Discovery Institute's Wedge Strategy (see appendix) where the ultimate objective is not to arrive at a scientific consensus regarding a better explanation of reality, but to win converts to a particular religious view. A religious view moreover which is intolerant of dissent, and in which 'truth' is a flexible concept that is handed down from the cult leadership to followers who are expected to acquiesce and defer to the cult leaders' authority in all things.

In other words, a far-right, hierarchical society in which democracy plays no part such as that which the democracies of the world fought to rid itself in the middle of the 20th century.

As was shown in the Kitzmiller case (6), claimed peer-reviewed papers supporting intelligent design and irreducible complexity turned out, on close inspection to be nothing of the sort. Professor Michael Behe was forced to admit under oath that a paper he co-authored with David W. Snoke (7), cited by Discovery Institute as a peer-reviewed paper supporting intelligent design by 'proving' irreducible complexity in an amino acid sequence, could actually evolve by accumulated point mutations in 20,000 years, or more quickly if other forms of mutation such as inversions, insertions, etc, were taken into account.

As Judge John E. Jones III[4] in his summing up of the Kitzmiller case, pointed out, every one of Behe's examples of

Introduction

'irreducible complexity' cited in his book, *Darwin's Black Box*, had been refuted by peer-reviewed papers but there were no peer-reviewed papers supporting it or intelligent design.

The Discovery Institute had feared the trial would be the disaster it turned out to be for the ID movement and its Wedge Strategy. It tried to wash its hands of the proceedings by withdrawing its expert witnesses, William A. Dembski, Stephen C. Meyer and John Angus Campbell. The Discovery Institute's, director Bruce Chapman also asked Behe and Minnich to withdraw, but they testified anyway, with disastrous results.

Creationism in all its disguises is as dead as astrology, alchemy, phlogiston and miasma and as useless as they are for explaining the observations and predicting the outcome of scientific experiments. It should be consigned to the rubbish tip for all primitive superstitions.

The following chapters will concentrate on the evidence from science that the TOE is alive and well and the fundamental basis for interpreting biological and geological data whereas there continue to be no peer-reviewed papers advocating for intelligent design creationism, which should by now be regarded as a theory in crisis, and dismissed as an idea that failed to generate any peer-reviewed support or provide anything useful to mainstream biology, cosmology, geology, physics or indeed any field of science, if only it qualified as a scientific theory in the first place.

---

[4] John Edward Jones III (born June 13, 1955) is the 30th President at Dickinson College and a former United States district judge of the United States District Court for the Middle District of Pennsylvania. He is best known for his presiding role in the landmark Kitzmiller v. Dover Area School District case, in which the teaching of intelligent design in public school science classes was ruled to be unconstitutional. A Republican, he was appointed by President George W. Bush) (Wikipedia)

In order to keep the narrative in reasonable flow, I have included technical details, definitions and brief biographical information in footnotes. Where indicated, an AI source (ChatGPT4o) was used to research background information on dating methods, geological formations and archaeological sites, etc.

As always, with my books, never take anything I say as definitive; always fact check! A comprehensive list of references is provided, many of which provide links to open access science papers.

The Evidence from Science

Creationists such as Stephen Myer and Michael J. Behe often cite complexity as evidence for intelligent design, although their reasoning never rises above the argument from ignorance incredulity, the god of the gaps and the false dichotomy fallacies

The argument from ignorance Fallacy:

Because something is currently unknown or even unexplained by the current state of knowledge does not mean it will never be known or explainable, so to jump the gun and to assume that the locally popular god did it, is premature and even immature, to say the least.

No previous gaps in our knowledge and understanding have ever needed a god to explain it and every gap closed by science has always been found to have a perfectly natural explanation. To assume that this particular god will prove to be an exception is simply a leap of faith and a pessimistic view of the scientific method of which any professional scientist should be ashamed

The God of the Gaps Fallacy:

Creationist's gods are invariably perfectly designed to fit the gaps they are traditionally inserted into. In effect, they are merely euphemisms for the gaps in their knowledge and understanding.

Much of creationist propaganda is manufacturing gaps in which to fit the locally popular god(s). The fallacy appeals particularly to those who need spurious confirmation of existing bias.

The Failure of Creationism

The False Dichotomy Fallacy:

This fallacy depends on persuading the target that there are only two choices – a particular science position or the religious one (and only the locally popular religion). The fact that, even **if** the current scientific view is proved to be wrong, there may well be alternative scientific explanations isn't allowed for in the argument. Again, this is not the position any self-respecting professional scientist would adopt.

Using those three fallacies, which is about the sum total of creationists arguments, the following examples of scientists showing no signs whatsoever of finding the scientific consensus on the definition and mechanisms of evolution inadequate to explain the facts and turning to creationist notions of intelligent design, complete with unproven magic entities acting in undefined ways, to be a better explanation. On the contrary, the idea that species evolve is basis to their understanding of what can be observed.

The first goes to the heart of Professor Behe's and Stephen Meyer's assumption that complexity needs a designer. It is an example of a layer of complexity evolving to compensate for the fact that an earlier evolved mechanism was sub-optimal – just what the utilitarian TOE would produce but the exact opposite of what an intelligent designer would produce.

In fact, the argument from complexity is a poor one because, as I showed in my book *The Unintelligent Designer: Refuting the Intelligent Design Hoax* (8) the hallmark of good, intelligent design is minimal complexity. Complexity, especially needless complexity, is the hallmark of unplanned, utilitarian evolution, where whatever works, no matter how sub-optimal, will be retained and increase in the species gene pool over time, providing it conveys and advantage, no matter how marginal.

An intelligent designer, especially one imbued with the characterises of the Christian god – omniscience and omnipotence – would foresee the problems that would arise, and scrap a sub-optimal design and start again.

In the following cases, I'll show that not only are basic creationist beliefs false but the main plank of the Discovery Institute's Wedge Strategy – to win over mainstream scientific support for the notion of Intelligent Design has been a monumental failure. In each case, the fact that the Theory of Evolution is taken for granted by the scientists should be readily apparent as the fundamental unifying idea in biology without which none of the observations make much sense – and a gap which ID is singularly inept at filling.

Case 1. New Information by Gene Duplication

Biologists working at Washington University in St. Louis were investigating an observed phenomenon where plants use two slightly different ways to achieve the same solution to a problem they share with animals which use only a single solution, and one moreover which still works in plants if one of the two is knocked out.

Why the duplication?

First, the problem, and this, if you accept the creationist clams of intelligent design for the moment, is a problem of the designers own making.

It is the fact that certain sections of DNA can 'jump' around in the genome – so-called 'jumping genes', or transposons. These can occasionally add to the genetic information by creating new genes with new functions, but they are equally likely to jump into the middle of an essential gene and break it, or they can land in a DNA section adjacent to a gene and inhibit the control mechanism.

There wouldn't be a problem if these jumping genes hadn't been designed to jump around in the first place, but their ability to do so is because of an evolved fault in the mechanism for DNA replication.

The solution adopted by both plants and animals, discovered by the group led by Professor Xuehua Zhong[5], a professor of biology in the faculty of Arts & Sciences at Washington University, (9) is to add a methyl group to the transposon, effectively silencing it. Methylation is part of the epigenetic control of genes of which more later.

Methylation in both animals and plants is achieved with enzymes of the chromomethylase group of proteins. In plants there are two similar proteins, CMT3 and CMT2. CMT3 adds a methyl group to transposons in sections of DNA known as CHG and CMT2 methylates CHH section transposons.

In this context, CHG and CHH are different sequences of the nucleotides where methylation can occur. CHG means a cytosine followed by any nucleotide except guanine with the third nucleotide being guanine. CHH means a cytosine nucleotide followed by any two nucleotides, either of which is a guanine.

Studying the plant *Arabidopsis thaliana*, Professor Zhong's team found that CMT3 lacks an essential arginine amino acid which, following a gene duplication event in the plant's evolutionary history around the time green plants were evolving. In fact, there were several gene duplication events producing CMT1, CMT2 and CMT3. CMT1 was later repurposed.

The amino acid arginine is essential for CMT3 to recognise CHG transposons but the presence of this amino acid in CMT2 is variable, but over time, free to mutate without

---

[5] Professor Xuehua Zhong's research focuses on epigenetic regulation of plant traits and environmental adaptation and how plants reprogram epigenetic landscapes in response to environmental changes to meet growth and survival needs.

detriment, being the product of a duplicated gene, it acquired a long protein 'tail' which gives it improved resilience to heat-shock. It is, however, still able to methylate CHH section transposons, so was retained as a form of work-sharing as the evolving genome became more and more complex

Professor Zhong's team found that by adding arginine back into CMT2, it could also methylate CHG transposons, making CMT3 redundant.

So, to summarise that, through evolution, a gene got duplicated so there were two copies each of which coded for an essential enzyme which performed the same function on two slightly different sections of DNA.

Then one of the copies mutated so the enzyme could only work on one section. Meanwhile, if it hadn't mutated it could have done what it was now taking two enzymes and two copies of the gene to do.

And all because DNA has these things that act a bit like parasites, being duplicated and sometime doing harm for no apparent benefit to anything, least of all its host.

The Theory of Evolution explain both why there is a problem to be solved and why there are two solutions to the same problem. The idea that this could be the work of a supreme intelligence is risible.

This of course, is an example of a layer of complexity being present in a pant cell because an earlier layer of complexity – the duplication of DNA and the entire genome in ever plant cell sometime goes wrong and created transposons. So, a layer of complexity in the form of the epigenetic system has been co-opted to mend that mistake.

Are we to believe intelligent design better explains that situation than utilitarian evolution acting without a plan? Intelligent design creationists want to tell school children that it does, so they can more easily dismiss other 'problems' for biology by simply shrugging their shoulders and assuming God must have designed it that way for a purpose beyond our understanding. In other words, to be satisfied with not knowing.

As I mentioned earlier, this methylation process is part of the epigenetic system, which creationists jumped on before they understood it because it seemed to show that something acquired after conception and even after birth, could be inherited, contrary to what Darwin thought, that 'traits' were inherited from parents and could not be changed after birth, as a 'rival' evolutionary theorist, Jean-Baptiste Lamarck[6] had proposed.

Of course, if Darwin was wrong about even one tiny little thing, the entire edifice of Darwinian evolution is utterly destroyed, and creationism wins by default [creationist quote mine alert!]

Epigenetics is as good an example of complexity in a cell as you could wish for so you might have expected Discovery Institute propagandists to have seized upon it with glee and dashed off half a dozen more books explaining how it is definitely evidence for the Christian god and proof that the Bible's account of creation in Genesis is real history and genuine science, so we should do away with democracy and put fundamentalist Christians in charge.

However, their silence on the subject, as with parasites, is deafening. They will have realised that, properly understood,

---

[6] Jean-Baptiste Pierre Antoine de Monet, chevalier de Lamarck (1 August 1744 – 18 December 1829), often known simply as Lamarck, was a French naturalist, biologist, academic, and soldier. He was an early proponent of the idea that biological evolution occurred and proceeded in accordance with natural laws.

epigenetics, is a major embarrassment for creationism, as I showed in *The Unintelligent Designer* (8).

First, we need to consider why epigenetics is needed in the first place:

Epigenetics is necessary because in multicellular organisms, any advantage of multicellularity is only realised by specialisation of cells and their arrangement into organs carrying out specialist functions. Many of these functions are only necessary in the first place because of multicellularity. Mammals need digestive, respiratory and circulatory systems to get oxygen and nutrients and remove waste to the cells too far removed from the surface to do it the way single-celled organisms do it – by direct exchange with their environment.

Evolutionarily speaking, multicellularity gave some organisms an advantage over others, but it came at a cost. One of the costs is the complex, error-prone system of epigenetics and the need to reset and start again with each new individual.

That's what it does, but why does it need to be done?

It is needed because, just like single-celled organisms, the cells of multicellular organisms inherit the entire genome of their parent cells regardless of their eventual function as specialised cells in specialised organs. Unless the unnecessary and unwanted genes are turned off there would be no specialisation and so no benefit from multicellularity. When cells start becoming generalised and doing other things they are called cancer.

So, what any ID model needs to explain is why any intelligent designer would arrange it so that all cells (with one or two limited exceptions) contain all the DNA of the entire organism when they only need a few special genes to function? Why is this complex system of epigenetics necessary in the first place? Why would an intelligent designer not design things so that as cells become specialised, they only get the DNA they need?

Instead, we have the ludicrous situation of almost every one of our 17 trillion cells, give or take a few billion, having our entire genome then needing a complex process for turning most of it off and another complex process for switching it all back on again starting from scratch in the newly–fertilised zygote.

In epigenetics we have a few exciting challenges for biology; for creationism we have as good an example as you can wish for of designer incompetence - prolific waste, needless complexity, a clear failure to plan ahead and needing to make the most of a bad job, and of a ludicrously complex 'solution' to a problem of its own making because, apparently, the designer lacked the wit to rethink the problem and start again.

The evolutionary explanation is perfectly simple, as one might expect. Multicellular organisms evolved from single-celled organisms and inherited the cell-replicating mechanism that had taken a couple of billion years to evolve. It might not have been the perfect solution, but it was better than what went before it, so all the descendants of that initial population are stuck with it and have evolved a clunky, near-enough-is-good-enough solution to the problems it caused.

How this can be described as intelligent design is quite beyond me. It requires definitions of 'intelligent' and 'design' that are unrecognisable and indistinguishable from the normal definitions of 'gross incompetence' and 'stupidity'.

For evolutionary biology, of course, epigenetics is as nice an example as you could wish for of the utilitarian, pragmatic nature of evolution, where Natural Selection can only act on the here and now and where any solution, no matter how sub-optimal, will be adopted if it gives an advantage. It is an example of how evolution has no reverse gear and cannot scrap a sub-optimal solution and start again with a better one, as any intelligent design process should be capable of.

Very many organisms remain single–celled of course, and very many remain prokaryote[7] rather than eukaryote[8]. Evolution does not have a plan and is not trying to achieve anything.

Case 2. Marine Snails Observed Evolving

Creationists will often demand that 'evolutionists' produce evidence of evolution being observed in a laboratory, either feigning ignorance of, or genuinely ignorant of the many experiments which do just that with fruit flies and the on-going Lenski experiment[9] with bacteria.

---

[7] A prokaryote is a single-cell organism whose cell lacks a nucleus and other membrane-bound organelles. The word prokaryote comes from the Ancient Greek πρό (pró), meaning 'before', and κάρυον (káruon), meaning 'nut' or 'kernel'....[P]rokaryotes are divided into Bacteria and Archaea. {Wikipedia)

[8] The eukaryotes [are] organisms whose cells have a membrane-bound nucleus. All animals, plants, fungi, and many unicellular organisms are eukaryotes. They constitute a major group of life forms alongside the two groups of prokaryotes... Eukaryotes represent a small minority of the number of organisms, but given their generally much larger size, their collective global biomass is much larger than that of prokaryotes. The eukaryotes seemingly emerged within the Asgard archaea and are closely related to the Heimdallarchaeia. (Wikipedia)

[9] The *E. coli* long-term evolution experiment (LTEE) is an ongoing study in experimental evolution begun by Richard Lenski at the University of California, Irvine, carried on by Lenski and colleagues at Michigan State University, and currently overseen by Jeffrey Barrick at the University of Texas at Austin. It has been tracking genetic changes in 12 initially identical populations of asexual *Escherichia coli* bacteria since 24 February 1988. (Wikipedia)

The Failure of Creationism

Their demand is an example of setting an impossible standard of evidence of science, apparently thinking creationism will win by default when science fails their test, without needing to supply a scrap of supporting evidence themselves.

And, of course, if science does what they demand, there is the instant 'Gotcha!' "You see! It needed intelligence to set up the experiment! I win!"

One thing that science can't replicate in a laboratory is an environment subject to the vagaries of the weather, a free circulation of air and a variable food supply. However, occasionally an example of just that situation presents itself as it did in 1988 when a small skerry[10] off the coast of Sweden in the Koster archipelago, suffered a catastrophic toxic algal bloom which exterminated the population of marine snails, *Littorina saxatilis*[11]. This created the opportunity to reintroduce the snails and observe how they evolved. The snails occur throughout their range in two ecotypes:

- *High-shore ecotypes*: Found in wave-exposed zones. These snails tend to have thicker, more robust shells to prevent being crushed by waves or predators like crabs.

- *Low-shore ecotypes*: Found in sheltered, less exposed zones. These snails have thinner shells, allowing them to move more easily and conserve energy in less turbulent environments.

---

[10] A small rocky island, often almost barren apart from marine algae and maybe lichens.

[11] *Littorina saxatilis* primarily inhabits rocky shores along the Atlantic coasts of Europe and North America. It can be found from the upper to mid-intertidal zones, enduring a wide range of environmental factors such as desiccation, salinity fluctuations, and temperature extremes during tidal changes. (ChatGPT4o)

The study was led by researchers from the Institute of Science and Technology Austria (ISTA) and the Norwegian Nord University. Their findings were published in the journal, *Science Advances* in October 2024 (10). They repopulated the skerry in 1991 with 700 snails from a predation-dominated environment to the wave-dominated skerry.

What they found was exactly what the Theory of Evolution by Natural Selection predicts – the snails diverged into the two ecotypes, each fitted for different zones on the tiny skerry.

As the team had predicted, there were transitions in shell size and morphology, changes in allele frequency at positions throughout the genome and chromosomal rearrangement frequences.

In other words, what the team found was that the snails evolved exactly as predicted according to the standard definition of evolution – change in allele frequency over time.

What creationists traditionally do at this point it to insist on a different definition of evolution – change from one taxon to an entirely different one – snails into bats; cows into rabbits, etc. which, if ever it did occur, would falsify the TOE.

Young Earth Creationists (YECs) are quite happy demonstrating intellectual bankruptcy by demanding evidence for something then moving the goal post when the demanded evidence of produced.

Intelligent design creationists are slightly more sophisticated but still suffer from the same problem of explaining these sorts of observed transitions in terms of intelligent design. They haven't yet decided whether intelligent design means continuous redesign as species adapt and to account for observed transitions in the geological column.

Did their intelligent designer design the stem species as a single act of creation then allow the processes of natural selection, genetic drift, etc to produce the changes over time, or is there a continuous process of new creations to account for the observed changes?

In other words, intelligent design creationists, while seeking to destroy 'Darwinism' have to implicitly incorporate it into their 'alternative' just to create a roll for their designer god in the process.

Incidentally, notice how the scientist who carried out this study had not the slightest doubt what the Theory of Evolution would predict and that it fully explained the observations. There is no evidence that they found the theory less than adequate for the task, or of the constantly predicted 'Demise of Evolutionary Biology'.

Case 3. Make Do and Mend

Readers familiar with the delightful designs of the English eccentric William Heath-Robinson[12], will readily appreciate the analogy of the Heath-Robinson designs found in nature.

No problem was too trivial, and no solution was too simple for William Heath-Robinson to design a needlessly complex solution. He would freely utilise everyday objects designed for one purpose for an entirely different one.

---

[12] William Heath Robinson (31 May 1872– 13 September 1944) was an English cartoonist, illustrator and artist who drew whimsically elaborate machines to achieve simple objectives. The earliest citation in the *Oxford English Dictionary* for the use of "Heath Robinson" as a noun describing any unnecessarily complex and implausible contrivance is from 1917. The phrase "Heath Robinson contraption" perhaps most commonly describes temporary fixes using ingenuity and whatever is to hand, often string and tape, or unlikely cannibalisations.

The Evidence from Science

For example, a grandfather clock standing on an upright piano. On top of the clock are four chairs balanced on two planks of wood, holding up a writing desk standing on an upturned table with a step-ladder on top of that, as a contraption for training mountaineers. The piano meanwhile needs a stack of books under one leg to make it level. And safety is provided by scattered mattresses, cushions and pillows.

Everything is held together by lengths of string, each of which has a knot in it because it had been made from scraps of string once used for something else.

Heath-Robinson's designs were inspired by wartime deprivation where nothing went to waste and everything was kept and recycled, and yet the whole thing looked as though it would work if ever it was built. It definitely looked intelligently designed for a meaning of the word 'intelligent' normally used for something stupid. And of course, if it were to be built, the fact of its needless complexity would render it error prone and dangerous to use.

Heath-Robinson contraptions are the exact opposite of that you would expect of an intelligent designer of the calibre envisioned by intelligent design creationists. They are, however, closely analogous to what you would expect of a utilitarian process making use of whatever is to hand to produce a utilitarian design, often incorporating things originally 'designed' for an unrelated function – the elements of the flagellar motor exapted from the Type III secretion system, for example.

An example of just such an error-prone Heath-Robinson contraption was discovered recently by a research team at the University of Würzburg. It is a workaround for a problem caused by the error prone method for replicating the entire genome in every cell where DNA is frequently broken and needs to be repaired.

It is an added level of complexity as so often, to compensate for something else that, had it been intelligently designed in the first place, would either not have been needed or at least would have worked as intended and without error – or it would have been scrapped and replaced with a better one.

The one crumb of comfort for creationists in this finding is that the solution involves some of the 'junk' DNA[13] that they deny exists. Junk DNA is so-called, not because it isn't transcribed into messenger RNA[14] (mRNA) but because it doesn't code for a protein. In this case the RNA itself is the functional unit. These non-coding RNAs are known as long non-coding RNA (lncRNA).

The University of Würzburg team has published the results of their investigations in the journal *Genes & Development* (11).

DNA damage can be either a single-strand break or a double-strand break. The latter is particularly dangerous as it can lead to a loss of genetic information. The type of break determines the response which involves specialised protein complexes. The process generally follows these steps:

Sensor proteins: These proteins detect damaged DNA. For example, ATM (Ataxia Telangiectasia Mutated) is primarily responsible for detecting double-strand breaks, while ATR (ATM and Rad3-Related) is activated by single-strand breaks and stalled replication forks.

Signal transduction: Once damage is detected, these sensors activate a cascade of signalling molecules that mobilize the repair machinery. Proteins like p53, Chk1, and Chk2 play key

---

[13] Deoxyribonucleic acid. The inherited, stored form of genetic information that is transcribed into RNA, the template for protein synthesis.

[14] Ribonucleic acid. The metabolically functional transcription of genetic information which carries the instructions for the amino acid sequence in proteins.

roles in coordinating this response by halting the cell cycle and facilitating repair.

Cells use different mechanisms depending on the type of break:

For Single-Strand Breaks: The base excision repair (BER) pathway is the main mechanism for fixing minor damage, like oxidative damage or small chemical alterations to the DNA.

The nucleotide excision repair (NER) pathway corrects larger, bulkier lesions such as those caused by UV radiation.

For Double-Strand Breaks, depending on the nature of the break:

Non-homologous end joining (NHEJ): This is a quick repair pathway that rejoins the broken DNA ends without needing a template. It's error-prone because it can introduce small mutations.

Homologous recombination (HR): This is a more accurate process that uses a sister chromatid (present after DNA replication) as a template to repair the break without loss of genetic information.

What Happens When Repair Goes Wrong?

1. Mutations and Cancer: If DNA damage is not properly repaired, it can lead to mutations—changes in the DNA sequence. These mutations can affect genes involved in cell growth and division (oncogenes or tumour suppressors), leading to uncontrolled cell proliferation and cancer. For example:

    - p53 mutations are very common in cancers and occur when the cell's ability to trigger apoptosis (cell death) after DNA damage is lost.

- BRCA1/BRCA2 mutations impair homologous recombination, leading to breast and ovarian cancers.

2. Genomic Instability: When cells can't repair DNA damage correctly, they accumulate mutations over time. This creates genomic instability, which is a hallmark of cancer cells. Genomic instability can lead to chromosomal rearrangements, duplications, or deletions, contributing to tumour progression.
3. Aging and Degenerative Diseases: Inefficient DNA repair is also linked to aging. Over time, as more DNA damage accumulates without being repaired, cells lose their ability to function properly. This can contribute to age-related diseases such as neurodegenerative disorders (e.g., Alzheimer's, Parkinson's).
4. Developmental Disorders: Some inherited diseases result from defects in DNA repair mechanisms:

    - **Xeroderma Pigmentosum (XP):** Individuals with XP have a defect in the nucleotide excision repair pathway, leading to extreme sensitivity to UV light and a high risk of skin cancers.
    - **Ataxia Telangiectasia (AT):** A defect in the ATM gene affects the ability to repair double-strand breaks, leading to neurodegeneration, immune system deficiencies, and cancer.

On the face of it a horrendously complex process for correcting something that, if it had been intelligently designed wouldn't need correcting. And fertile ground no doubt for an intelligent design creationist to discover another example of 'irreducible complexity' in a layer of complexity that should not have been necessary anyway if intelligently designed.

So, back now to what the team from Julius-Maximilians-Universität Würzburg discovered:

The team found that the lncRNA, NEAT1 (nuclear enriched abundant transcript 1) which is found in high concentrations in cancer tumours is also involved in DNA damage detection and repair. They found that NEAT1 become methylated in the presence of damaged DNA.

Methylation is a control mechanism that changes the shape of the lncRNA molecule and is a way the cell controls the activity of lncRNA similar to the epigenetic process for controlling gene expression. This causes NEAT1 to accumulate at the site of DNA damage and so act as a signal to initiate the repair process.

NEAT1 doesn't actually repair the broken DNA but controls the release of an RNA-binding DNA repair factor.

A ramshackle, overly complex solution to a problem of which William Heath-Robinson would have been proud, A problem that should not have arisen if cell division and replication of DNA had been designed the way an omnipotent, omniscient intelligent designer would have designed it – unless it intended the process to randomly fail and cause cancer, of course.

Case 4. Doing the Same Thing in Two Different Ways.

A characteristic of evolved systems, where there is no mechanism for exchanging ideas and using a solution to a problem in one species to solve the same problem in an unrelated species, is that solutions to the same problem tend to be different in different taxons.

Evolution by natural selection is quite capable of evolving mechanism for something like flight, multiple different ways, and even when the solution involves wings, the wings will have different structures for different major taxa – birds, bats, insects.

But what is slightly unusual is this example of two populations of the same species of plant evolving two entirely different solutions to the same problem. It was discovered by three researchers from the Universitat Autònoma de Barcelona (UAB) Plant Physiology Lab. in collaboration with researchers from the University of Nottingham (UK), the Max Planck Institute for Biology (Germany), and Charles University in Prague (Czech Republic). The team have recently published their findings in *Proceedings of the National Academy of Science (PNAS)* (12)

They were investigating how the plant, *Brassica fruticulose*, a relative if the cabbage, *Brassica oleracea,* rape, *Brassica napus* and more distantly mustard (*Sinapis alba*), has adapted to be able to grow on costal soil subject to inundation by sea water and sea spray and so with a high salt content.

The plant is common around the Mediterranean and grown near Barcelona where it occurs as two different populations. The team discovered that these populations have evolved entirely different ways to solve the same problem.

Those from the north (Cap de Creus region) are able to restrict root-to-shoot sodium transport, preventing the damage of the aerial parts. In contrast, those from the centre accumulate sodium in the leaves, but they use efficient mechanisms of osmotic adjustment and compartmentalisation that allow them to tolerate high concentrations of this compound.

If creationism were a proper science, it should be able to formulate a plausible mechanism for this difference, but the only response possible is that God did it that way for reason we can't understand. In other words, the 'answer' provided by creationism is, "Just be content with not knowing because you wouldn't understand anyway".

The evolutionary origins of this in two separate species is probably too obvious to be spelled out but it is an interesting example of allopatric speciation and stimulated the question, what would happen if the two populations came into contact? Would one form replace the other, would they hybridize and produce a range of intermediates having a non-viable inheritance and if so, would barriers to hybridization arise resulting in two different, non-interbreeding populations?

Creationism, on the other hand, makes no predictions or testable hypotheses and serves only to suppress further enquiry, and questioning a god's motives or competence it tantamount to heresy.

Case 5. New Genetic Information Arising Naturally

A major theme of intelligent design creationism is the claim that new genetic information cannot arise naturally so requires intelligent intervention.

As usual though, how a creator god goes about creating this new information and inserting it in a species genome remains unexplained and supporters of ID creationism are expected to be satisfied with not knowing – "God can just do things like that, so we don't need to concern ourselves with how, when or where."

The argument is the main claim to fame of Discovery Institute fellow, William A. Dembski but his argument and particularly his definitions have evolved over time in response to scientific objections.

His argument briefly runs as followed:

Specified complexity: using this ill-defined but impressive-sounding assertion, Dembski asserts that genetic information displays complexity (therefore intelligence is required) and is highly specified for a particular function, so showing the use of intelligence in the design. However, how this claim can be tested is never spelled out, we just have to accept Dembski's word for it, and it remains subjective.

This is a classic argument from incredulity and a god of the gaps false dichotomy fallacy; a gap which has been intelligently contrived.

Dembski attempts to reinforce this subjective claim with an appeal to a fundamental law of science- the Law of Conservation of Energy, which Demski misapplies to genetic information.

However, even if that misapplication of thermodynamics was valid for genetic information, considering that no biologist would ever claim the chemicals that make up DNA spontaneously pop into existence *de novo*, there is no violation of the Laws of Thermodynamics when new sections of DNA are inserted into the genome of a species, just as there is no violation of those laws when DNA is replicated. New DNA is produced at every cell division so new genetic information arises trillions of times in the development of every embryo and the growth of every organism. Dembski would have us believe that when a new strand of DNA is being replicated, if, say, a guanine molecule gets inserted into the new strand in place of a cytosine molecule, there is a violation of one of the Laws of Thermodynamics that would not have been violated if the cytosine molecule had been inserted. This is nonsensical, of course, but makes his disinformation look like real science.

Dembski then invokes the 'improbability' argument and again fills this contrived gap with his god. Basically, he argues that it is highly improbable that a specified sequence could arise spontaneously, conveniently forgetting the iterative nature of evolution over time and the effects of selection in the process. Selection gives the process a high degree of direction in favour of improved function over time.

Dembski also conveniently forgets that evolution takes place over time in the gene pool of a population, not in a single cell as a single process. Many of the fundamental process that operate at the level of the cell evolved in ancient eukaryote ancestors in populations of trillions over hundreds of millions, even billions of years, in a highly competitive environment in which anything which gave a small advantage would quickly spread through the population.

In such a gene pool, with a generation time often measured in minutes or hours. the billion to one chance would be a regular occurrence. Nor do metabolic pathways need to evolve in any particular sequence, since multiple pathways can be evolving independently in parallel, not in sequence.

In other word's Dembski's improbability gap is contrived.

Dembski also argues against natural selection as being capable of creating new information. This is a classic straw man fallacy because no-one suggests the act of selection somehow creates the new information. Selection causes the new information to spread throughout the gene pool, if it gives the carrier a competitive advantage. How the new information arises is a different matter.

Lastly, Dembski employs the familiar false equivalence fallacy by comparing biological systems with human artifacts (a version of the Palley's Watch argument that Darwin and Wallace refuted in 1859). The simple fact is that human artefacts do not self-replicate in a selective environment so there is no natural mechanism for creating them. And we know who creates human artefacts and how they created them, so there is no need to invoke an unproven magic deity to explain them. For a detailed rebuttal of the 'Palley's Watch' false equivalence fallacy, see by blog post, *The Teleological Fallacy or Paley's Broken Watch* (13)

But Dembski himself seems to be aware of the shortcoming and fallacies in his argument, as they have evolved over time in response to criticism by proper scientists and a general rejection of his claims by mainstream science.

His first attempt was in his 1998 book, *The Design Inference* in which he introduced the two terms in the context of genetic information:

- Complexity - Events or patterns that are highly improbable (low probability under chance hypotheses). Subjective, poorly defined and untestable.
- Specification: Patterns that exhibit an independently given structure or function, recognizable without referencing the event itself. Again, subjective, poorly defined and untestable.

He suggested a three-step process for detecting 'design':

1. Eliminate deterministic explanations (regularities). How?
2. Assess whether the pattern is highly improbable under chance. How? Allowing for iteration and selection of assuming it all happened as a single event?)
3. Identify if the pattern fits a specific, recognizable "specification." Whose specification? Specification for what?

Then, in his 2002 book, *No Free Lunch* his argument has evolved:

- He introduced a more formalized mathematical treatment of *specified complexity* based on conditional probabilities.
- He articulated the concept of the *universal probability bound* (10^{-150}) as a threshold for determining when complexity is beyond the reach of natural processes, combining cosmological, chemical, and biological improbabilities. (Again, no recognition of selection acting in the gene pool and the same assumption that it all happened as a single event in a single cell).
- He emphasized that specification requires a *functionally significant pattern*, not just any pattern. For example, a functional gene or protein sequence was considered specified. In other words, calculating the probability of something that has happened, like dealing several hands of 13 cards then calculating the probability of dealing exactly those hands in that order and concluding that dealing cards is next to impossible.)

By the mid 2000's in response to continuing criticism his argument has evolved further:

He now relies on a parody of natural selection, categorising it as a 'search for a search' as though natural selection is sentient and goal-orientated, and he now has a model for natural selection that required an 'infusion of information' in order to achieve its goal of functional complexity (his new term for 'specified complexity').

And today it has evolved to include a new definition of specification. That is now tied to '', functional utility – a working protein or a meaningful message, with the same assumption of a goal. Now the argument isn't that natural selection can't evolve 'complex specificity'; nowadays natural selection can only evolve specified complexity if it has some pre-existing 'active information' added by an intelligent entity. And still, he offers no way to quantify the amount of information in a genome.

Does repeating a length of DNA add to the information or does it simply repeat the same information? Does the sentence, "The cat sat on the mat" have half the information of "The cat sat on the mat. The cat sat on the mat", or the same information?

And still the argument depends on the parody version of natural selection as a sentient, goal-seeking process.

But the biggest argument against Dembski's attempt to construct an argument that 'proves' Darwinian evolution doesn't work because new genetic information can't be created is the simple fact that it runs counter to reality. New genetic information does arise in a genome and has been seen to do so, not by a magic process involving intelligent supernatural entities but by well understood natural processes that require nothing more than the operation of the basic laws of chemistry and physics.

New information can arise in a genome by gene or even whole genome duplication, by horizontal gene transfer; or by hybridization, for example. And what Dembski fails to recognise is the difference between information and meaning. This subtle difference is usually lost on creationists, but take, for example a situation where a mutation means an organism is now the color of sand instead of being black. If the organism lives in a dark cave, that mutation would be meaningless; if, however, that organism lived on a sand-coloured background, being sand coloured would give it a competitive advantage in being harder for a predator to spot. The mutation has been given meaning by the environment, not with any other 'highly improbable' change in the information.

Another hypothetical example could be a mutation giving a bacterium the ability to use polypropylene as a fuel source. 200 years ago, that mutation would have been meaningless;

The Evidence from Science

today it would be hugely beneficial to the bacterium. The presence of polypropylene in the environment gives a completely different meaning to the same information.

To use the analogy of information being contained in a sequence of letters, consider the two strings of letters, 'INFORMATION' and 'TEAVE'.

Which has the most information to you? Is 'teave' a typo for 'leave' or 'tease' maybe?

Now, assuming you are an English speaker and not Latvian, type 'teave' into Google Translate and ask it to translate it from Latvian to English.

In fact, 'teave' is Latvian for 'information'. The two letter sequences have different amounts of information but the same amount of meaning, depending on how the environment translates the information into meaning.

As, I said, the fatal flaw in Dembski's argument - no new information arising without magic – is that it is at odds with what can be observed – new information arising in a genome without magic.

An example of this was published recently in the journal *Molecular Biology And Evolution*. It was written by four researchers working at the University of Arkansas who discovered a novel way in which new information can arise in a genome. Their discovery bridges the gap between entirely new gene formation from noncoding regions and the more traditional model in which new functions can arise from duplicated genes.

They examined the evolution of antifreeze proteins in fish — an essential adaptation that allows fish to survive in freezing waters by preventing ice formation through the binding of their antifreeze proteins to ice crystals.

The team investigated these proteins in three unrelated fish lineages and uncovered surprising results. While the proteins in each lineage are functionally and structurally similar, they evolved independently from different genetic sources. This phenomenon, known as convergent evolution, represents a rare case of protein sequence convergence. It demonstrates how the same adaptive traits — and even nearly identical protein sequences — can be produced through entirely different evolutionary trajectories. In each case, rather than arising by mutation and repurposing of duplicated genes, the new genes arose *de novo* by mutations in non-coding (for protein) sections of DNA (part of the so-called 'junk' DNA).

To be effective, the proteins produced all need to bind to ice crystals to prevent them forming larger crystals in the fishes' blood. The strengths of the selection pressure came from it being a matter of life or death in a changing environment in which sea level glaciation was starting to occur as Earth went into a new Ice Age.

These findings show that new genes can form by repurposing fragments of ancestral genes while incorporating entirely new coding regions of DNA. Contrary to the claims by the Discovery Institute fellow, William A. Dembski.

Horizontal Gene Transfer

As well as genes arising *de novo* within the non-coding sections of DNA and by repurposing duplicated genes by mutation and natural selection in the population gene pool over time, there is a quicker and more immediate way for organisms to acquire new genetic information, often in the form of fully functional genes evolved over time – horizontal gene transfer from another species, sometimes from an unrelated taxon altogether.

The fact that genes acquired this way is testament to the commonality of the genetic code as well as the mechanism for translating the DNA template into messenger RNA (mRNA) and the translation of that into the amino acid sequences of the proteins the gene codes for.

Horizontal gene transfer can come from viruses, for example, especially the group of viruses known as retroviruses because they insert a DNA template of their RNA into the genome. Over time, these can lose their viral 'function' by mutation, and they are then available to be repurposed.

Examples of these endogenous retroviruses can be found in the same location of the same DNA in fish, amphibians, reptiles and mammals, showing how these taxons form nested hierarchies strongly indicative of descent with modification from common ancestors.

Examples of endogenous retroviruses providing the basis for new genes are:

Syncytins and Placental Development: Syncytins are proteins derived from retroviral envelope genes that have been repurposed by mammals for placenta formation. These proteins play a critical role in the fusion of cells to form the syncytiotrophoblast, a layer essential for nutrient exchange between the mother and foetus. Without these endogenous retroviruses, placental mammals might not have evolve.

Examples: Syncytin-1 in humans is derived from the HERV-W retrovirus and Syncytin-2, also in humans, comes from the HERV-FRD retrovirus.

Innate Immunity: Endogenous retroviruses (ERVs) contribute to the regulation of the immune system. They have been implicated in immune responses, such as:

- The production of antiviral peptides.
- Regulation of interferon responses.

Example: In mice, MuERV-L retroviral elements help regulate the activation of the zygotic genome during early embryonic development.

Neural Development and Function: Retroviral elements have contributed regulatory sequences that influence the expression of nearby genes, including those involved in brain development and function.

Example: Human endogenous retrovirus K (HERV-K) sequences are active in certain neurons and may play a role in neural plasticity.

Genetic Diversity and Evolutionary Innovation: Retroviral integrations often generate genetic variability, which can lead to the evolution of new functions.

Example: Retrotransposons derived from retroviruses, such as LINE-1, have driven genome restructuring and the evolution of new genes.

Resistance to Pathogens: Some retroviral-derived genes have been co-opted to protect against viral infections.

Example: The Fv1 gene in mice, which provides resistance to certain retroviruses, is derived from an ancient retroviral capsid protein.

Epigenetic Regulation: Retroviral insertions have provided regulatory elements such as promoters, enhancers, and silencers, influencing the expression of genes.

Example: In primates, HERV-derived regulatory sequences modulate the expression of genes involved in immune responses.

These examples of horizontal gene transfer from viruses illustrate how retroviruses have shaped genomes, providing new genetic information that has been co-opted by hosts for various beneficial functions.

But horizontal gene transfer is not just from viruses. Genes can be (and have been) acquired from other sources and perhaps the record in this respect is held by the strange but abundant marine micro-organism, the bdelloid rotifers.

These are microscopic multicellular eukaryote organisms that are all female and breed parthenogenically by a form of cloning. This presents the species with a problem for long term survival in that there is no genetic crossover as found in sexually-reproducing organisms, so no opportunity for new combinations of genes to arise.

This is believed to reduce a species evolvability making them prone to extinction if their environment changes and is believed to be the reason so few species are parthenogenic – which, on the face of it, would seem to give them a reproductive advantage and the ability to found new colonies with a single individual.

And yet bdelloid rotifers display a high degree of genetic diversity!

The rotifers appear to have solved this problem by acquiring genes from bacteria and other microbes.

As a team of researchers from the University of Oxford, the University of Stirling and the Marine Biological Laboratory (MBL), Woods Hole, MA USA, they use a battery of defences so acquires when attacked by fungi. The team recently published their findings in *Nature Communications*. The surprise discovery was that, using these genes, rotifers are able to manufacture antibiotics – not an ability normally associated with eukaryotes.

That rotifers have been doing this for millions of years is evidenced by the fact that some of the acquired genes have been modified when compared to those found in bacteria. Some of the acquired bacterial genes have given rotifers the ability to bypass the normal ribosomal[15] way of constructing

---

[15] The ribosomes are cell organelles that 'read' the information in

amino acid chains using an RNA template, and to assemble short amino acid chains, or 'non-ribosomal' peptides[16] directly.

Horizontal gene transfer tends to be between a parasite and its host. For example, as a team led by Tappei Mishina at the RIKEN Center for Biosystems Dynamics Research discovered, a parasitic nematode which infects mantises then turns them into zombies that jump into water and drown so the parasite can reproduce, can do so because it has acquired a mantis gene and modified it. This means the host's immune system doesn't recognise as foreign the protein the worm produces that controls the insects' behaviour. Their work was published in *Current Biology*. (14)

In another example, a team from the University of Maryland School of Medicine's (UMSOM) Institute for Genome Sciences (IGS) found that a species of fruit fly, *Drosophila ananassae*, has the entire genome of a *Wolbachia* bacterium embedded in its genome. Their findings were published, open access, also in *Current Biology*. (15)

The last example of horizontal gene transfer – there are many more in the scientific literature, comes from a team of researchers at the University of Sheffield, UK. They discovered that the evolution of grasses included frequent horizontal (or lateral) gene transfer, the effects of which were to enable them to grow taller and faster. This is a natural version of genetic modification. The research is reported in the journal *New Phytologist*. (16)

---

mRNA and use it to build a protein chain from amino acids.
[16] A short chain of two or more amino acids.

Case 6 Evidence of Common Ancestry

An important principle for formulating a scientific explanation that creationists habitually ignore is the requirement that the explanation for a phenomenon be as simple as possible because the simplest explanation - the explanation requiring the least number of steps and the smallest number of entities is most probably the correct explanation.

A chain of causality has no need to take detours or have more links in it than necessary. For example, a stone falls to the ground when we drop it because of one cause and one cause only – the force of gravity and Earth being by far the larger mass, the stone falls towards it while any movement of Earth towards the stone is infinitesimal.

We could add all manner of whimsical forces and entities in that explanation, such as angels competing in a tug-o-war in which the angel on the ground always wins. We could propose that the stone is sentient and can receive instructions telling it which direction to move in, and we can invent all manner of fanciful alternative explanations for why a stone falls to the ground when we drop it, but we can only prove one of those – the force of gravity – and that explanation provides a complete explanation (at least with what we know of gravity).

And this is what creationists do when they insist on inserting their god in the explanation for anything for no better reason that they want it to be there, or they need to give it credit for something.

The principle was formalized by William of Ockham or Occam[17] who formalised it as:

---

[17] William of Ockham or Occam (c. 1287 – 10 April 1347) was an English Franciscan friar, scholastic philosopher, apologist, and Catholic theologian, who is believed to have been born in Ockham, a small village in Surrey. He is considered to be one of

The Failure of Creationism

Entia non sunt multiplicanda praeter necessitatem (do not multiply entities needlessly).

This is known as Occam's Razor, also called the principle of parsimony or the law of parsimony.

In my falling stone example, the needless entities are the angels, a sentient ability and something or someone to issue the instructions. None of them add to the explanations and in fact add another level of complexity to it because now we need to explain the origin of the angels, why we can't see them, how they pull on the stone, and we have to explain how a stone can be sentient and most of all we have to explain the entity giving the instructions, how they are conveyed, etc.

Using Occam's Razor, we should pare away all those needless entities because we can't establish the truth of any of them, so all that remains is the force of gravity, and the least complicated (most parsimonious) answer is the result.

What creationists invariably do, is insert an unproven entity (a god) into the explanation which, more often than not is complete without one. William A. Dembski, for example, now appears to accept that a species genome changes over time, but insists an intelligent agent of some sort must have supplied 'an infusion of information' in order for the genome to know the goal it is evolving toward (or is it so the environmental selectors know in which direction to drive the evolving genome? He isn't clear on that point.

However, the mechanisms for *de novo* genes to arise is well known and understood as is the action of environmental selectors in giving direction to the evolving genome, not

---

the major figures of medieval thought and was at the centre of the major intellectual and political controversies of the 14th century. He is commonly known for Occam's razor, the methodological principle that bears his name, and also produced significant works on logic, physics and theology.

toward some childish parody - goal-seeking evolution - but simply towards greater fitness in that selective environment.

Working to a correct definition of evolution, Occam's Razor will pare away unproven gods and 'infused information' and so provide the most parsimonious explanation for why the genome of a species tends towards greater fitness in its environment, but not, of course for why evolution produces some imaginary pre-determined 'specified complexity. Because that isn't a component of the Theory of Evolution and no serious biologist believes evolution is a goal-seeking process, that doesn't require an explanation.

Dembski has merely manufactured a gap and provided the least parsimonious 'explanation' for no better reason than for somewhere to sit his god (and to sell book to people looking for gaps in which to sit their god).

An example of creationists failing to use Occam's Razor can be seen in their frequent attempts to dismiss evidence of common ancestry in the form of structures or metabolic pathways in common, or at least based on common ancestry, by claiming they are evidence of a common designer.

This would be slightly more plausible if only there weren't so many examples in nature of different solutions to the same problem, unless one accepts that a common designer is also an amnesiac who forgets what it designed earlier and designs afresh.

So, in the following example, if the argument is 'common designer' we should apply Occam's Razor and pare away the unnecessary common designer because the explanations that evolutionary biology can supply are not improved with it and are simply rendered less parsimonious.

The example was provided by researchers in the College of Natural Science at The University of Texas at Austin who discovered that two proteins known as viperins and argonautes, which are found in eukaryotes, including all multicellular organisms, are structurally very similar to viperins and argonautes found in Asgard archaea[18]. The team recently published their findings, free access, in the journal *Nature Communications*. (17)

These proteins serve the same anti-viral function in both Asgard archaea and eukaryotes and are thought to have originated as the result of arms races between archaea and virus in the early years of the evolution of prokaryotes. Arms races are something I will touch on later, but for now, evolutionary arms races are powerful drivers of evolution for bath a parasite and its victim, so it is not surprising that these antiviral proteins arose very early on, and, being essential in the presence of viruses, it is not surprising that they have been retained and remain highly conserved throughout the evolution of eukaryote by endosymbiosis with an Asgard archaea ancestor and during the long evolution of multicellular eukaryotes such as humans.

Significantly, however there **are** differences, recording the passage of time and reflecting the greater complexity of the eukaryotes. This raises the obvious question for advocates of a common designer, why the differences?

The researchers showed that, in archaea, when viperins detect foreign DNA, which might indicate a dangerous virus, they edit the DNA so that the cell can no longer make copies of it, which stops the virus from spreading. When argonautes detect foreign DNA, they chop it up, also halting the virus. Additionally, in more complex organisms, argonautes can block the virus from making proteins in a process called RNA silencing. The University of Texas at Austin team showed

---

[18] Asgard or Asgardarchaeota is a proposed superphylum belonging to the domain Archaea that contain eukaryotic signature proteins. It appears that the eukaryotes, the domain that contains the animals, plants, and fungi, emerged within the Asgard, in a branch containing the Heimdallarchaeota. {Wikipedia)

that this mechanism, previously only known in bacteria, was also present in Asgard archaea.

The study of Asgard and Eukaryote viperin provides valuable insights into the evolution of antiviral defence mechanisms. The presence of similar antiviral proteins in both archaea and eukaryotes suggests that these defence strategies are ancient and have been conserved throughout evolution.

While both Asgard and Eukaryote viperin share functional similarities, their specific roles and mechanisms may differ due to the differences in their cellular environments and the types of viruses they encounter.

So, a question for intelligent design creationists: if these functionally very similar proteins do the same thing in archaea and humans (and all other eukaryotes) why are they different?

If the answer is that they have adapted over time as the eukaryotes evolved into multicellular organisms, is this an evolutionary process, or a serious of new creation *de novo* events which just happens to look like a progressive one?

Case 7. 'Macro-Evolution' in Just 36 Years

Many creationists try to change the standard definition of Evolution – change in allele frequency in a population gene pool over time – to one in which there are two different sorts of evolution – micro-evolution and macro-evolution to make it easier to attack 'macro-evolution' by pretending it's a type of evolution where a species turns into an entirely new taxon in a single event.

It's nonsense, of course and is repeated so frequently and corrected so often that creationists can't fail to know they are attacking another straw man parody and demanding science provides evidence for something science doesn't claim happens.

The Failure of Creationism

Scientists use the terms 'micro-evolution' and 'macro-evolution' not because the underlying processes that cause them are different, but because it is often necessary to distinguish between the small steps by which evolution progresses and the large accumulations of change lots of small changes can add up to over time.

It is not a matter of different processes but a difference in the extent of evolution, like walking a step at a time and walking a mile into town. For some reason, creationists seem to believe the former is perfectly possible but the latter is impossible because it has to be done in a single stride.

When I first became involved in the science vs creationism debate in the 1980's in the early days of user forums and bulletin boards, having got over the initial surprise that there really were grown adult who still believed in Noah's Ark, Adam & Eve, and a literal magic creation of the universe from nothing just a few thousand years ago, the official dogma of the creation cults was that evolution didn't happen, ever, because it was impossible, due to the Second Law of Thermodynamics – a mantra that was repeated endlessly by people who clearly had no idea what either evolution is or what the Second Law of Thermodynamics says.

It then slowly dawned on the cult leaders that there were far too many species in the world, and even more if you count all the extinct species, for two (or seven) of each species to spend a year on a wooden boat, needing food and water and some means of disposing of the byproducts of eating and drinking, so they hit up the idea of conceding that 'micro-evolution' was not only possible and definitely not forbidden by the 2LOT, but happened at an unimaginably fast rate after the animals left the ark, where only two (or seven) of each 'kind' had been cooped up for a year.

The problem for that daft notion is that for say a cat 'kind' to mushroom into all the different cats in the world would require whole new breeding populations of new species arising spontaneously every year for a few hundred years, then magically slowing down to an undetectable pace just as people began to take an interest in nature in the 19th century.

The humorous things is, though, that one species giving birth to another, as is now regularly required for all species that left the Ark and their descendants for a few hundred years, is an example of the very 'macro-evolution' the fiction was created to hive off into an impossible parody.

But of course, as with just about all creationist objections to science, the facts are against them on the matter of 'macro-evolution' as they define it (evolving new structures or processes that distinguish it from its predecessor, so placing it in a new taxon). The instances, apart from the usual examples of speciation by hybridization are long slow processes occurring in populations often widely separated. No one sees and records a 'macro-evolution'.

The late, great philosopher, Daniell Dennet, author of *Darwin's Dangerous Idea*, used the analogy of an isthmus becoming an island by a process of erosion. At what point does it qualify as a separate island? When the sea covers the neck of land joining it to the mainland at high tide, when it covers it at low tide or only when it still covers it at the lowest of low tides?

But with species diverging, there may be a prolonged period when the diverging populations can interbreed as they go through a sub-species stage. Some populations may never progress to full population status because there will always be frequent gene flows between the two populations.

In nature, the mechanisms of population divergence don't produce sharp delineation between related species but for the convenience of taxonomy, we try to fit them into one classification or another, to draw sharp lines where the reality is fuzzy.

But that's digressing from the point here that so-called 'macro-evolution', defined as new structures of new processes, does occur and can occur very quickly, and has been seen to occur.

A spectacular example of this was witnessed in a population of Italian wall lizards, *Podarcis sicula*. In 1971 a bunch of scientists, intending to observe how a population of the Italian wall lizard, *Podarcis sicula*, adapted to a new environment, transferred just five males and five females from the small Croatian island of Pod Kopiste in the southern Adriatic Sea, to the nearby island of Pod Mrcaru. And there they stayed while Yugoslavia fragmented and descended into warring factions.

Thirty-six years later another group of scientists visited the island, where they discovered that not only had the teeming descendants of the relocated lizards replaced and apparently exterminated the former resident species, *Podarcis melisellensis*, on Pod Mrcaru, but that they had also diverged considerably from the original population on Pod Kopiste.

That they were indeed the descendants of the original founder population was confirmed by analysis of their mitochondrial DNA[19], which was identical to those on Pod Kopiste.

These findings were published in 2008 in PNAS (18), since when any supposed 'scientist' employed by the creation industry to write disinformation about science, should have been aware of this discovery, had they been keeping up to date with developments in their supposed field of expertise, so when they claim it doesn't happen, they are either lying or showing professional incompetence.

---

[19] Mitochondria have evolved from endosymbiotic cyanobacteria and have retained some of their original DNA. Because sperms contribute no mitochondria to the zygote all mitochondria are inherited from the female so mitochondrial DNA can be used to trace the female line through evolutionary history.

The Evidence from Science

The main physical and behavioural changes the scientists found were:

The major significant changes were:

- A change of diet. The Pod Mrcaru lizards now eat mostly plant material, not the insects their ancestors ate.

- To cope with this different diet, the Pod Mrcaru lizards have a measurably larger head which allows for more powerful jaw muscles and a more powerful bite, needed to bite the plant matter into small chunks for swallowing and digestion.

- The Pod Mrcaru lizards are less territorial and less aggressive than their ancestors because they no longer need to defend a territory to ensure enough insects. This has enabled a much higher population density. They are also less active.

- To digest the vegetarian diet, the Pod Mrcaru lizards have developed caecal valves in their intestines. These slow down the flow of food through the digestive system and act to turn sections into fermentation vats to break down the plant cell walls.

This latter is the most dramatic morphological change since only 1% of lizard species have caecal valves. It amounts to a new structure in this species, evolved in just 36 years. All the changes are the result of changing from an insectivore to an herbivore.

Significantly too in relation to the forlorn claim that 'Darwinism' is about to be overthrown and replaced by intelligent design, complete with its unproven magic and unexplained supernatural entities working in mysterious ways, the scientists have this to say in the abstract to their paper:

"Here we show how lizards have rapidly evolved differences in head morphology, bite strength, and digestive tract structure after experimental introduction into a novel environment. Despite the short time scale (≈36 years) since this introduction, these changes in morphology and performance parallel those typically documented among species and even families of lizards in both the type and extent of their specialization. Moreover, these changes have occurred side-by-side with dramatic changes in population density and social structure, providing a compelling example of how the invasion of a novel habitat can evolutionarily drive multiple aspects of the phenotype." (18)

Absolutely no sign there then that the biologists found the observations couldn't be explained by the Theory of Evolution, and this paper becomes yet another in the mountain of supporting evidence for it.

There are now many examples of relatively rapid large-scale changes in morphology in a population. For example, in May 2007, Michael A. Bell, Windsor E. Aguirre and Nathaniel J. Buck published an account of rapid change in a population of sticklebacks, *Gasterosteus aculeatus,* in an Alaskan lake. (19) Sticklebacks are an essentially marine coastal species that frequently enters rivers and small streams and finds its way into lakes where it can establish a new colony. Following the extermination of the population in Loberg Lake, Alaska, the lake was repopulated with a fresh invasion between 1983 and 1988.

First a little background information:

Stickleback fish exhibit distinct lateral plate morphs in their populations. These morphs are encoded by variations in the *Eda* (ectodysplasin) gene. The three main lateral plate morphs are:

1. Fully-Plated: bony plates cover most of the body, from head to tail. These are found primarily in marine populations or in freshwater populations where predation is high. The plates provide protection against predatory fish and provide structural reinforcement aiding mobility when under attack.

2. Partially-Plated: bony plates are present but cover only part of the body (typically the front half). These are found in intermediate freshwater environments where predation pressure is moderate. The advantage in these environments is that although mobility and protection is reduced, this is offset by the reduced energy cost of building the full plate.

3. Low-Plated Morph: the plate is typically restricted to a small cluster near the head or absent altogether. This morph is common in low-predation freshwater environments, particularly in lakes and streams. The advantage in these environments is enhanced swimming agility due to reduced weight and improved energy efficiency, allowing resources to be redirected to growth and reproduction.

In summary: high predation in marine and certain freshwater environments favours fully-plated morphs, while low-predation conditions favour reduced plating. Producing bony plates is energetically expensive, and in predator-scarce environments, it is selected against.

The morphs are largely controlled by alleles of the *Eda* gene in which the High-expression allele produces fully-plated phenotypes, the Low-expression allele, produces low-plated morphs.

These changes are reversible if the fish return to a high-predation or marine environment, giving the stickleback phenotypic plasticity, which is itself an advantage and probably the reason neither of these alleles reaches fixation in a population.

Annual samples of the stickleback population in Loberg Lake were taken between 1990 and 2001 revealing a rapid evolution in the lateral plate (armour). The 1990 sample was almost monomorphic for the complete plate morph, but by 2001, the frequency of completes had declined to 11%, and lows had increased to 75%. The partial plate morph and two unusual intermediate plate phenotypes were generally rare.

Relating that back to the standard definition of evolution as change in allele frequency in a population over time, this is a classic example of evolution. It also complies with the creationist definition of 'macro-evolution' in that there was a change in morphology involving a structure. And it was observed over a period of just 12 years.

Lastly, we have the example of field experiments in which founder populations of a species of lizard, *Anolis sagrei,* were introduced to small islands that different in terms of vegetation from the original population's island. Over a period of 10-14 years, the populations differentiated rapidly from each other and from the original population. The degree of differentiation was directly related to the degree of difference in vegetation on the different islands. This experiment is described in a paper published in *Nature.* (20)

Findings such as this are usually the cue to creationists to move the goal posts and redefine 'macro-evolution' to something no biologist ever suggested – e.g., sticklebacks turning into frogs or sharks, or lizards growing wings and flying, in other words to jump from one branch of the evolutionary tree to another branch entirely, something which if it ever happened would actually falsify the Theory of Evolution.

The same creationists can never raise their claim to the same standard of evidence they demand of science, by providing evidence of a god creating a species *de novo* from soil. The reason is probably all too obvious.

Case 8. 'Non-Existent' Transitional Fossils

The creationist literature and creationist groups in the social media are full of claims that 'transitional forms' have never been found, yet what you can never find is a scientific definition of the term 'transitional' in the context of an evolving species. One way to kill a debate with a creationist who has just made that claim, is to ask them what they would expect a transitional fossil to look like. To answer that would violate the creationist unspoken rule that one should never give an answer which can be tested.

The claim depends on the childish parody of evolution which sees it as an individual of one species turning into an unrelated species via a short series of intermediates – a cat turning into a dog by first growing a dog's head on a cat's body, then a dog's tail and legs, etc, and finally a dog's body, etc.

In other words, it comes from the creationist need to constantly redefine terms such as 'evolution', 'change over time', and even 'transition' to explain away evidence that refutes their beliefs.

However, when we relate the process of evolution to the standard definition of change in allele frequency in a population over time, it should be obvious that every fossil is a snapshot of that process at a point in time and no individual in that population will ever display the complete history of the changes to that point in time.

Many evolutionary changes will not be captured by most fossilisation processes, which usually preserved the hard parts such as bone and teeth, but rarely the soft parts and with only a very few recent exceptions, changes in DNA. It's difficult to imagine any fossilisation process that would preserve the underlying changes in proteins and metabolic pathways, all of which are part of the evolutionary process.

This insistence by creationists on seeing 'transitional forms' probably comes from their belief that, it you can prove Charles Darwin wrong in the slightest degree, the entire body of science they call Darwinism will collapse and be utterly defeated. It comes from Darwin's, perhaps slightly optimistic statement and with characteristic honesty and integrity:

> "Geology assuredly does not reveal any such finely graduated organic chain; and this, perhaps, is the most obvious and gravest objection which can be urged against my theory. " (21)

But with an equally characteristic dishonesty and lack of integrity, creationists neglect to point out the context of their quote mine. Darwin was, as was his style, setting out the perceived problem before explaining how his theory solved it.

What Darwin actually said was:

> "The main cause, however, of innumerable intermediate links not now occurring everywhere throughout nature depends on the very process of natural selection, through which new varieties continually take the places of and exterminate their parent-forms. But just in proportion as this process of extermination has acted on an enormous scale, so must the number of intermediate varieties, which have formerly existed on the earth, be truly enormous. Why then is not every geological formation and every stratum full of such intermediate links? Geology assuredly does not reveal any such finely graduated organic chain; and this, perhaps, is the most obvious and gravest objection which can be urged against my theory.

> "The explanation lies, as I believe, in the extreme imperfection of the geological record.
>
> "In the first place it should always be borne in mind what sort of intermediate forms must, on my theory, have formerly existed. I have found it difficult, when looking at any two species, to avoid picturing to myself, forms DIRECTLY intermediate between them. But this is a wholly false view; we should always look for forms intermediate between each species and a common but unknown progenitor; and the progenitor will generally have differed in some respects from all its modified descendants."

In effect, what Darwin is saying here is that we should **not** expect continuous series of fossils for every extant species but when we **do** find fossils, they should be somewhere on a continuum from an ancestral species and the current form, and not, as creationists keep demanding evidence of and intermediate between two extant species as though one transitioned into the other.

So, where are these 'missing link' transitional forms?

In fact, every fossil is a transitional form just as Darwin predicted, but there are some notable stem species showing how earlier forms diverged to give two related taxons, for example, a recent fossil, exquisitely preserved with enough fine detail to show it is at least close to the progenitor of spiders, scorpions and horseshoe crabs.

It was described in a paper published recently in *Current Biology* (22) by a research team from Yale University.

The fossil, *Lomankus edgecombei*, a Megacheiran, was found in 'fool's gold' (iron pyrites) in central New York, in a geological formation known as Beecher's Bed. The process of pyritization, which is a rare fossilisation process, preserves soft tissue structures in exquisite detail, by replacing them with sulphates as they decay.

Beecher's Trilobite Bed, located in upstate New York, is an extraordinary fossil site within the Ordovician Frankfort Shale, a rock formation dating back about 450 million years. Discovered in the late 19th century by palaeontologists Charles Beecher, it's renowned for preserving trilobites with incredibly detailed soft tissue, a rarity in the fossil record.

The trilobites from Beecher's Bed are fossilized in pyrite (fool's gold), which has preserved not only their exoskeletons but also delicate, soft body parts, including legs, antennae, and gills. This unique preservation is likely due to the low-oxygen, sulphide-rich environment where the organisms were rapidly buried, preventing decay.

In the pyritization process the pyrite replacement occurred as iron and sulphur from the surrounding sediment reacted with the organic matter, replacing the original tissues. This rare process has left the fossils with a golden, metallic sheen, adding a striking visual aspect to their scientific value.

The fossils allow scientists to see trilobite anatomy and gain insight into their lifestyle. For example, the presence of complex appendages and delicate structures indicates they were likely agile bottom-dwellers.

Beecher's Bed is a valuable resource for studying Ordovician ecosystems, evolutionary biology, and taphonomy (the process of fossilization). It has led to a better understanding of the early marine environment and trilobite behaviour.

Lomankus edgecombei is the only known Megacheirans to have survived beyond the Cambrian into the Ordovician by which period all the Megacheirans were thought to have gone extinct.

It is now incumbent on creationists to say why this fossil and many more fossils of similar ancient ancestral species should not be considered to be exactly what Darwin was talking about.

Another example of a transitional species from close to the diversification of two major taxons was described recently by researchers co-led by Martin R. Smith and Emma J. Long, from Durham University's Earth Science Department and Jie Yang and Xiguang Zhang of the Institute of Palaeontology and Yunnan University, China. Their findings are published in *Nature*.

It's clear to anyone who looks at them that insects and segmented worms have a common origin in that they have a segmented body plan, but to a creationists appearances prove nothing and anyway they will always claim it as evidence of a common designer and demand to see the transitional form as evidence, then reject it because it doesn't disprove their claim.

But it answers their demand for an example of a transitional form. as they diverge from the segmented worms and was dated by one of the most accurate and least error-prone geochronological methods we have – U-Pb dating of zircons from volcanic tuffs. I describe this dating method in *Refuting Creationism: Why Creationism Fails In Both Its Science And Its Theology* (23) but briefly, zircon forms crystals in volcanic magma as it cools and, because they are physically similar to zircon atoms, uranium atoms can be included in the crystal lattice, but importantly lead atoms can't be. So, when pristine at the time they form zircons will contain a small amount of uranium, so of which will be radioactive (^{236}U and ^{238}U). Both those isotopes of uranium have long half-lives and decay via a decay chain of intermediate isotopes, mostly with very short half-lives, to stable, non-radioactive isotopes of lead (Pb).

The result is lead atoms in the zircon crystals that could only have got there by radioactive uranium being incorporated when the crystal was formed. So, by simple arithmetic, by measuring the amount of lead and uranium in the zircons, we can work out how long ago the crystals were formed.

For the technically-minded, the simple formula for calculating the age of the zircons is:

$$t = \frac{1}{\lambda} ln\left(1 + \frac{D}{P}\right)$$

Where:

> t is the age of the sample.
>
> λ is the decay constant of the isotope (related to its half-life).
>
> D is the number of daughter atoms (e.g., lead).
>
> P is the number of parent atoms (e.g., uranium).
>
> ln is the natural logarithm.

In that way the research team were able to accurately date the fossils to the Cambrian.

This fossil, which the team named *Youti yuanshi,* belongs to a group called the euarthropods, which includes modern insects, spiders and crabs.

Despite being no bigger than a poppy seed, the 3D fossil reveals the larva possessed an advanced brain, digestive system, circulatory system and clusters of nerves extending into primitive legs and sensory appendages. It helps bridge a key transitional gap in arthropod evolution between simple worm-like ancestors and the successful modern arthropod body plan.

In particular, the fossil's brain anatomy reveals pivotal steps in how the arthropod head and its appendages like antennae, jaws and eyes became segmented and specialised over time from ancestral brain regions.

The researchers highlighted the fact that the fossil fills an important gap in our understanding of how the arthropod body plan originated and became so successful during the Cambrian Explosion of life.

Again, we have the complete dependence on the Theory of Evolution to fully explain the observations with no hint that one involving an unproven supernatural designer might provide a better explanation. Quite simply, this transitional species was designed by a natural process of environmental selectors acting on inherited variation. No magic required.

Of course, what creationists are really interested in is 'proving' there are no 'transitional fossils' showing how modern humans evolved from the same ancestral species as modern chimpanzees, so these fossils are normally the subject of concerted disinformation campaigns which question everything from the dating methods used, to the honesty, integrity and motives of the scientists who discover and report on them,

One such example is that fossilised near perfect foot os a juvenile *Australopithecus afarensis* – the species to which the famous 'Lucy' was assigned and a species believed to be, if not immediately ancestral to the *Homo* genus, then a close cousin species to the Australopithecine that was.

The fossil was found at Dikika, Ethiopia in the same general area of Africa as 'Lucy' and a re-examination if the foot shows a remarkable mosaic of modern and archaic features. The bones of the ankle show the species walked upright but the big toe was mobile so it could still be used for climbing trees, at least during childhood.

Now, if a creationist could be persuaded to break cover and come clean on what they would expect their supposed 'missing link' or 'transitional form' to look like, I can't think of anything that could be called 'transitional' that isn't a mosaic of what it evolved from and what it evolved into.

The Failure of Creationism

Only a child could be persuaded that evolution means a population of Australopithecines with Australopithecine feet would suddenly start giving birth to fully-formed modern humans with a fully-formed modern human feet without intervening generations showing gradual change to various parts of the feet over time.

The researchers from several American universities and research institutions presented their evidence in the journal *Science Advances*. (24)

Continuing with the same theme of transitional Hominin fossils, we have an almost complete skeleton of *Australopithecus sediba* (25) with its chimpanzee-size brain, lower limbs that are almost indistinguishable from those of *Homo sapiens* and the upper limbs of a chimpanzee until you look at the hands that are far more like those of *H. sapiens* than those of a chimpanzee.

In fact, it's another classic example of a mosaic of archaic and modern human features exactly what we should expect of a transitional species sitting somewhere in the hominin family tree, midway between an Australopithecine and a *Homo*.

I once showed a creationist who repeatedly insisted there were not transitional forms showing humans evolved from an ape, a picture of an *Au. sediba* skull and pictures of the skulls of a modern human, a chimpanzee and a gorilla, and asked him whether it was the skull of a human or of an African ape. "It's an extinct ape!" he declared. I then showed him pictures of an *Au. sediba* hand and the hands of a human, a chimpanzee and a gorilla and asked him whether the hand was that of a human or an African ape. "It's a human hand, obviously!" he declared, "I can even tell it's the hand of a manual labourer!".

When I showed him a picture of the complete *Au. sediba* skeleton and asked him to explain why an extinct African ape would have the hands of a human manual labourer, he promptly left the debate group. In all probability he's still active in other creationist groups, asserting that there are no transitional forms.

When I did the same with another fanatical creationist some months later, to howls of laughter (or its online equivalent) he declared that he didn't care whose skull it was because "Everyone knows *Australopithecus* is an extinct Australian ape!".

He also quickly left the group and deleted his account.

The truth of the matter is that, rather than there being no transitional fossils, there are, if that is even possible, too many of them. As more are discovered it is becoming more and more obvious that the history of human evolution in Africa was not that of a linear progression from *Paranthropus*[20] through the Australopithecines and a progressively more modern series of *Homo* species, but a history that include many side branches, some of which ended in dead ends and others that merged back into the main hominin branch. For long periods, there were two, three or more coexisting species or subspecies, some of which interbred after spending a long period of genetic isolation.

And it looks like this process continued as first *H. erectus* left Africa and spread across Eurasia, diversifying into geographical variants as it did so, followed some million or more years later by one or more waves of *H. sapiens*. These newcomers then interbred with the descendants of *H. erectus* – Neanderthals and Denisovans - to produce the genetic diversity found in non-African *H. sapiens*, which, despite the

---

[20] *Paranthropus* is a genus of extinct hominin which contains two widely accepted species: *P. robustus* and *P. boisei*. However, the validity of *Paranthropus* is contested, and it is sometimes considered to be synonymous with *Australopithecus*. They are also referred to as the robust australopithecines. They lived between approximately 2.9 and 1.2 million years ago (mya) from the end of the Pliocene to the Middle Pleistocene.

ingression of Neanderthal and Denisovan genes is still less diverse than the genes of African peoples.

Some African groups have more genetic diversity that the whole of the non-African population, for the simple reason that they started with a larger population and have been evolving for far longer than the few tens of thousands of years that non-African human have been.

The evidence for this lies not so much in the transitional fossils that so frequently turn up, but in the genomes of living people each of whom carries the transitional fossils of their ancestor in their genome.

If those transitional forms are not convincing evidence that there are indeed transitional forms, because they don't show 'transition' from chimpanzees, we have, *Sahelanthropus tchadensis* (26) considered by many to be either the common ancestor of *Homo* and *Pan* or a close relative of it.

Sahelanthropus tchadensis lived about 7–6 million years ago. Fossil evidence of *Sahelanthropus*, notably the skull nicknamed *Toumaï*, was discovered in Chad in 2001. Chad in sub-Saharan Africa lies within the area known as the Sahel, a fertile area south of the Sahara Desert that forms a natural corridor between East and West Africa. *Sahelanthropus* means Ape of the Sahel

It contains a mix of primitive and derived traits, such as a small brain (around 360–370 cc, similar to modern chimpanzees, a relatively flat face with reduced prognathism (less protrusion of the jaw compared to apes) and evidence suggesting it may have walked upright (bipedal), based on the position of the foramen magnum (the opening in the skull for the spinal cord).

It is fair to say that there is not a general consensus about where, if at all, this species fits on the hominin evolutionary tree. There is also an ongoing debate about whether

The Evidence from Science

Sahelanthropus walked upright as the foramen magnum suggests.

However, at the point in evolution where species are actively diverging there is bound to be a lack of clarity about exactly how far that divergence has progressed. The fact that there is a dispute about *Sahelanthropus*'s status is what we would expect of a stem species or one very close to it.

While this book was in preparation a paper was published which refutes a number of creationist claims. It refutes the claim there are no transitional forms in the fossil record, that there is no evidence for common ancestry and descent with modification and it refutes the notion that Earth is a mere 6-10,000 years old.

It also refutes the false claim that the 'Cambrian[21] Explosion' was an instantaneous creation of complex body plans, without ancestors.

And of course, it refutes the claim that scientists are abandoning the Theory of Evolution in favour of creationism.

The paper by geologists led by Professor Mary Droser, from the University of California, Riverside (UCR), announced the discovery of a small worm-like *Uncus dzaugisi*, making it the oldest known ecdysozoan, in the fossil record and the only one from the Precambrian period.

A characteristic of this group of animals is that they all have a hard exoskeleton which they shed periodically as the grow, putting nematode worms, insects, arachnids such as spiders, scorpions and horseshoe crabs, crustaceans and scalidophora[22]

---

[21] The Cambrian is the first geological period of the Palaeozoic Era, and the Phanerozoic Eon. The Cambrian lasted 53.4 million years from the end of the preceding Ediacaran period 538.8 Ma (million years ago) to the beginning of the Ordovician Period 485.4 Ma. (Wikipedia).
[22] Scalidophora is a group of marine pseudocoelomate ecdysozoans

in the same large clade, one of the largest clades in the animal kingdom.

Biologists have long hypothesised that just such a stem organism should have existed, and this discover confirms this prediction the Theory of Evolution.

The first author of the paper, Ian Hughes, a marine biology graduate from Harvard said, "Like many modern-day animal groups, ecdysozoans were prevalent in the Cambrian fossil record and we can see evidence of all three subgroups right at the beginning of this period, about 540 million years ago. We know they didn't just appear out of nowhere, and so the ancestors of all ecdysozoans must have been present during the preceding Ediacaran[23] period". The team's paper was published in the journal *Current Biology* (27).

The usual response of creationists to news such as this is to try to cast doubt on the dating method used or the integrity of the geologists/palaeontologists. First a little background on the 'Ediacara Member', from where the team report the fossil being found:

> The Ediacara Member is a significant geological formation located in South Australia, particularly within the Flinders Ranges. It is part of the Rawnsley Quartzite and is named after the Ediacara Hills, where some of the world's most famous early multicellular fossils have been discovered. These fossils date back to the Ediacaran Period, approximately 635 to 541 million years ago, a critical time in Earth's history that predates the Cambrian explosion of life.

---

that was proposed on morphological grounds to unite three phyla: the Kinorhyncha, the Priapulida and the Loricifera. (Wikipedia).
[23] The Ediacaran is a geological period of the Neoproterozoic Era that spans 96 million years from the end of the Cryogenian Period at 635 Mya to the beginning of the Cambrian Period at 538.8 Mya. (Wikipedia)

The Ediacara Member is globally renowned for its exceptionally preserved fossils of soft-bodied organisms. These are part of the "Ediacaran biota," which include some of the earliest-known complex life forms, such as, *Dickinsonia*, a flat, segmented organisms resembling leaves or discs, *Spriggina,* a worm-like creatures considered potential precursors to arthropods and *Charniodiscus:*, a frond-like structures anchored to the seafloor.

It is composed predominantly of quartzite, with layers of sandstone and siltstone. These sedimentary rocks were likely deposited in shallow marine environments, including tidal flats and lagoons, offering excellent conditions for fossil preservation. (ChatGPT4o)

It was dated using a combination of U-Pb dating of zircon crystals in ash beds and volcanic tuffs (see page 58), stratigraphic correlation[24] and palaeomagnetic studies[25]. U-Pb dating is, as I have said before, one of the most accurate and least error-prone dating methods available since the probability of contamination by uranium or leakage of lead from the crystal lattice is minimal.

Case 9. Closing in on Abiogenesis

Judging by the nonsense and the childish challenges creationists keep throwing about in the social media,

---

[24] The Ediacara Member is part of the 'Rawnsley Quartzite' which lies above the Cryogenian ('Snowball Earth') glaciation and the Cambrian. (ChatGPT4o)

[25] Sedimentary rocks can preserve the Earth's magnetic field orientation at the time of their deposition. Paleomagnetic data from the Ediacara Member have been used to support its age by correlating its magnetic signatures with the global geomagnetic polarity time scale (GPTS) for the late Precambrian.

creationists have a strange idea about abiogenesis. The phrase, "you can't get life from non-life" is constantly chanted like a protective mantra, but what on earth do they think life is?

It is as though they think there is some magical ingredient called 'life' that needs to be inserted into inorganic chemicals before they can be 'alive' but challenged to define this 'life' or even to say whether it is a substance, a process, or something else like a force unknown to science, it is impossible to get an honest answer.

I often liken it to the squawk of a trained parrot who can make the noises in response to trigger sounds but has no idea what they mean to a human listening.

Of course, 'life' is simply what we call the physiological processes that distinguishes us from a dead body. At death, the body's physiology ceases due to the failure of the respiratory and circulatory systems to deliver nutrients and oxygen to our brain.

As a former paramedic I can attest that, if we can restore circulation and respiration quickly enough to prevent irreversible damage to the brain, the body's physiology can be restored to 'life'. In other words, 'life' is a process, the ultimate purpose of which is to resist entropy by using the energy in nutrients to fuel metabolic processes.

All living matter is comprised of a few elements, mostly carbon, hydrogen, nitrogen and oxygen with some sulphur, phosphorus and iron. None of those elements contain anything magical that, when they join together into larger molecules such as proteins, nucleic acids, ATP, etc. acquire something that distinguishes them from the carbon, oxygen, nitrogen, etc, that can be found in a handful of garden soil. They are just bog-standard atoms and molecules. What turns them into living substances is the organised metabolic processes inside cells.

The Evidence from Science

So, the challenge for biochemists is to explain how those organised cells arose in the first place, not where some magic ingredient called 'life' came from.

And to turn those cells into self-replicating organisms that form the foundation of evolutionary biology because as soon as we have replication with variation, evolution will inevitably result and all that's then needed is time, and Earth has had vast amounts of time since it coalesced from an accretion disc around the forming sun some 3.8 billion years ago.

The problem creationists create for themselves comes from mistaking religious dogma for scientific facts, so when they claim it is impossible to create 'life' from 'non-life', they are not stating some immutable scientific law like the Third Law of Thermodynamics that basically says energy is not creatable or destructible, but a dogma.

All that a sweeping statement like that needs by way of refutation, is a plausible, irrefutable mechanism by which it could happen. Whether or not it actually happened that way is irrelevant to the claim that it is impossible. A plausible mechanism that can't be refuted is proof that it is possible.

One is tempted to ask what they imagine happens when the dead food they eat gets converted into living substances through the process of digestion and assimilation, if as they claim, this is impossible without the addition of some magic 'life'. In fact, I have frequently tried to get an answer to that simple question but one is never forthcoming. It's probably not too hard to work out why.

What is disappointing though is that no creationist has ever had the integrity to admitted they hadn't ever thought of that and needed to rethink their position as it was clearly wrong. You can never accuse a creationist of having too much honesty or intellectual integrity.

And of course, since 'life' is biochemical processes, there are no basic laws of physics or chemistry that forbid it, so, inevitably it is possible.

The question for science is then how?

At this point, a quote from Charles Darwin might be apposite:

> "Ignorance more frequently begets confidence than does knowledge; it is those who know little, and not those who know much, who so positively assert that this or that problem will never be solved by science."
>
> Charles Darwin

In my book, *What Makes You So Special: From the Big Bang To You* (28), I set out a ten-stage process by which life could have arisen in the most likely candidate location – deep ocean hydrothermal vents, sometime called 'black smokers' because of the sulphurous compounds that well up from cracks in the ocean floor. My list was based on a similar list by Nick Lane and Michael Le Page, published in New Scientist and attempted to answer the question of how the first self-replicating, free-living organisms arose:

> The honest answer to this question, like the question of how the first simple self–replicating molecule arose and what it was, is that we do not yet know. We do not know if it was a single line of development or two or more that later got together. However, laboratory experiments have come up with a very plausible series of steps, as outlined in a New Scientist article by Nick Lane and Michael Le Page (29). They assumed that the most likely location for it to have happened was in porous rocks in alkaline waters around geothermal vents and outlined ten steps:
>
> 1. Water filtering down into newly–formed rocks around geothermal vents reacted with minerals to

produce an alkaline, hydrogen and sulphide rich fluid that welled up in the vents.

2. This fluid reacted with acidic sea water which was then rich in iron to form deposits of highly porous carbonate rock and a foam of iron–sulphur bubbles.

3. Hydrogen and carbon dioxide trapped in these bubbles reacted to make simple organic molecules such as methane, formates and acetates; reactions that would have been catalysed by iron–sulphur compounds.

4. The electrochemical gradient between the alkaline fluid in the pores and the acidic seawater would have provided energy to drive the spontaneous formation of acetyl phosphate and pyrophosphate. These behave like ATP (adenosine triphosphate) which powers modern cells. This power supply would in turn power the formation of amino acids and nucleotides.

5. Currents produced by thermal gradients and diffusion within the porous carbonate rock would have concentrated the larger molecules creating the conditions for building RNA, DNA and proteins and creating the conditions for an evolutionary process where molecules that could catalyse the formation of copies of themselves would quickly dominate and win the struggle for resources.

6. Fatty molecules would have coated the surface of the pores in the rock, enclosing the self–replicating molecules in a primitive cell membrane.

7. Eventually, the formation of the protein catalyst, pyrophosphatase enabled the protocell to extract more energy from the acid–alkaline gradient. This enzyme is still found in some bacteria and archaea.

8. Some protocells would have started using ATP as their primary energy source, especially with the formation of the enzyme ATP synthase. This enzyme is common to all life today.

9. Protocells in locations where the electrochemical gradient was weak could have generated their own gradient by pumping protons across their membrane using the energy released by the reaction between hydrogen and carbon dioxide, so producing a sufficient gradient to power the formation of ATP.

10. he ability to generate their own chemical gradient freed these protocells from dependence on the pores in the rock, so they were now free to become free–living cells. This could have happened at least twice with slightly different cells, one type giving rise to bacteria; the other to archaea.

The above ten–step process is of course speculative and probably impossible to test and verify in a laboratory because the conditions around these geothermal vents deep below the ocean would be impossible to replicate in a laboratory, as would the time it might have taken. No–one is claiming it all happened in a day or two, or even weeks or years; not even the lifetime of a working scientist. It could have taken tens or hundreds of millions of years. No–one was in any hurry and there was no objective. Things happened when they happened. And when it happened, the inevitable process of evolution had something to work on.

I'll look now at some recent research that shows the sort of progress science is making in filling yet another god-shaped gap in creationists' understanding.

In February of this year, scientists at University College London, led by Professor Matthew Powner, showed that a molecule, pantetheine, which is the functional unit of one of the basic enzymes involved in cell metabolism - Coenzyme A - could be produced in water at room temperature. (30)

This was something of a breakthrough as previous attempts to created it by simulating the conditions on early Earth had failed. The difference was that in earlier experiments, the researchers used acid chemistry whereas Professor Powner's team used energy-rich nitriles.

Pantetheine is a small molecule derived from pantothenic acid (vitamin B5) and cysteamine. Its structure includes a diphosphate group, a cysteamine residue, and a beta-alanine residue. Pantetheine plays a crucial role in metabolism as a component of coenzyme A (CoA), which is an essential cofactor in numerous biochemical reactions, particularly those involved in the synthesis and breakdown of fatty acids, as well as the metabolism of carbohydrates and proteins.

Pantetheine would have played an important part in emerging life because it is involved in several essential processes:

> Synthesis of Fatty Acid - Fatty acids are crucial components of cell membranes and play roles in energy storage. Without the ability to synthesize fatty acids, early life forms would have been unable to create the lipid bilayers necessary for cellular structure.

> Energy Metabolism - Coenzyme A's is involved in energy production pathways such as the citric acid cycle and fatty acid oxidation which would have been necessary for the metabolism of early organisms, allowing them convert nutrients into energy to drive other metabolic processes
>
> Manufacture of Essential Molecules - Coenzyme A is also involved in the manufacture of various essential molecules besides fatty acids, including sterols, isoprenoids, and neurotransmitters. These molecules are crucial for cellular structure and function.

In the study, published in the journal Science (30), the research team created the compound in water at room temperature using molecules formed from hydrogen cyanide, which was likely abundant on early Earth.

This piece of research also showed that life could have originated in water which was believed by some to be too destructive for the essential molecules to form in. It had been proposed that life originated in water that was subject to frequent drying. The work also dispels the myth that Pantetheine is too complex to have been formed from simple ingredients and probably needed living organisms to manufacture it.

Driving the reactions that produced pantetheine were energy-rich molecules called aminonitriles, which are closely chemically related to amino acids, the building blocks of proteins and of life. The same team has previously used aminonitriles to produce peptides (short chains of amino acids) and nucleotides, the building blocks of DNA.

One of the problems abiogenesis needed to overcome was producing stable chains of amino acids (peptides[26]) in an

---

[26] Peptides are short chains of amino acids linked by peptide bonds. A polypeptide is a longer, continuous, unbranched peptide chain.

The Evidence from Science

aqueous medium that might be expected to have broken the peptide bonds that link the amino acids together.

This was shown to be possible on pre-biotic Earth by a research team at Purdue University led by Professor R. Graham Cooks who showed that the peculiar properties at the surface of water droplets, where, because electrostatic forces align the waterer molecules it behaves as though it is extremely dry (31). This is the same phenomenon that causes the surface tension on water.

Water droplets are everywhere in nature from raindrops to the spay from waterfalls and trickling streams to coastal sea spray and wave action.

Now, Professor Cooks who showed that the peculiar properties at the surface, working with Lingqi Qiu, now shown that these conditions apply at the larger centimetre scale as water evaporates on, for example, rocks on the margins of hydrothermal pools. They have also shown that, in the presence of oxazolones[27]. The reactions also preserve the chirality[28] of the amino acids so the resulting peptides are 'L' enantiomers[29], as found in all living organisms.

Polypeptides which have a molecular mass of 10,000 Da or more are called proteins. Chains of fewer than twenty amino acids are called oligopeptides, and include dipeptides, tripeptides, and tetrapeptides. (Wikipedia)

[27] Oxazolone is a chemical compound and functional group, with the molecular formula $C_3H_3NO_2$. It was named in-line with the Hantzsch–Widman nomenclature and is part of a large family of oxazole-based compounds. (Wikipedia)

[28] Chirality is a property of asymmetry important in several branches of science. The word chirality is derived from the Greek χείρ (kheir), 'hand', a familiar chiral object. An object or a system is chiral if it is distinguishable from its mirror image; that is, it cannot be superimposed onto it. Conversely, a mirror image of an achiral object, such as a sphere, cannot be distinguished from the object. A chiral object and its mirror image are called enantiomorphs (Greek, 'opposite forms') or, when referring to molecules, enantiomers. A

Explaining the significance of their work in their published paper in *Proceedings of the National Academy of Science* (32) the authors said:

> This study provides experimental evidence identifying oxazolones as the key intermediates in prebiotic peptide synthesis. These compounds yield the dipeptides upon reaction with water and generate tripeptides in the presence of other amino acids. These key steps in protein formation occur in pure water droplets. Amino acid chirality is preserved in forming the oxazolone and the addition of amino acids during peptide chain extension shows a strong chiral preference, viz. the aqueous droplet chemistry represents a simple route to chirally pure polypeptides. A direct connection between this intermediate and the dipeptide isomer, oxazolidinone, is demonstrated by simple hydration/dehydration. The oxazolone/oxazolidinone-mediated mechanism also occurs in macroscopic wet–dry cycling, establishing a strong connection between macroscopic and microscopic peptide synthesis.

---

non-chiral object is called achiral (sometimes also amphichiral) and can be superposed on its mirror image... [In chemistry,] a chiral molecule is a type of molecule that has a non-superimposable mirror image. The feature that is most often the cause of chirality in molecules is the presence of an asymmetric carbon atom. (Wikipedia)

[29] In chemistry, an enantiomer (from Ancient Greek ἐνάντιος (enántios) 'opposite', and μέρος (méros) 'part') – also called optical isomer, antipode, or optical antipode – is one of two stereoisomers that are non-superimposable onto their own mirror image. Enantiomers are much like one's right and left hands; without mirroring one of them, hands cannot be superposed onto each other. No amount of reorientation in three spatial dimensions will allow the four unique groups on the chiral carbon (see chirality) to line up exactly. The number of stereoisomers a molecule has can be determined by the number of chiral carbons it has. (Wikipedia)

So, we now have an explanation for how peptides and proteins with the right chirality could have formed on the pre-biotic Earth by the simple operation of the laws of physics and chemistry.

But, in order to function as discrete units, able to control the exchange of materials and energy with their environment, and most importantly, to establish an electrical gradient between the proto-cell and its environment which can be used to power metabolic processes. Without a cell membrane there would just be a soup of organic molecules, The question is, how did this form?

This problem for any theory of abiogenesis was solved by a team from Newcastle University, Newcastle-upon-Tyne, UK, led by Dr Graham Purvis, who showed that the basic units for making a membrane can be made in the conditions which exist in geothermal hot springs.

These basic units consist of long-chain amphiphilic[30] molecules, such as fatty acids, and the Newcastle team have shown that a range of functionalised long-chain aliphatic compounds, including mixed fatty acids up to 18 carbon atoms in length can be produced in a laboratory by mimicking the conditions in a geothermal hot spring with dissolved hydrogen and bicarbonate with the iron-rich mineral magnetite under conditions of continuous flow and alkaline pH even at relatively low temperatures (90 °C).

The reason these molecules are important is because they can form a two-layers membrane with the hydrophilic part on the outside and the hydrophobic part holding the structure together on the inside.

---

[30] An amphiphilic molecule has both hydrophilic (water loving) and hydrophobic (water rejecting) regions. Examples are soap and detergents.

By replication crucial aspects of the chemical environment found in early Earth's oceans and the mixing of the hot alkaline water from around certain types of hydrothermal vents in their laboratory. They found that when hot hydrogen-rich fluids were mixed with carbon dioxide-rich water in the presence of iron-based minerals that were present on the early Earth it created the types of molecules needed to form primitive cell membranes.

The team's research findings were published a few days ago in the journal, *Nature Communications Earth & Environment* (33).

It has long been assumed that living things began to self-replicate when they developed RNA capable of autocatalysis that is, catalysing the production of more copies of itself. Once a self-replicating molecule arose, the process of evolution by natural selection would have refined the process by adding layers of complexity to it. One of those layers of complexity was to store the information in RNA in the form of DNA, which today can be seen as RNA's date base.

RNA is still active in several cell metabolic pathways and carries the information which codes for protein enzymes and structural proteins.

But how did RNA first arise?

This question was answers by Quoc Phuong Tran, Ruiqin Yi and Albert C. Fahrenbach working at the University of New South Wales, Sydney, Australia, who found that a small addition to the formose reaction[31] would make it catalyse the formation of the building blocks of RNA, ribonucleotides.

---

[31] The formose reaction, discovered by Aleksandr Butlerov in 1861, and hence also known as the Butlerov reaction, involves the formation of sugars from glycolaldehyde and formaldehyde. The term formose is a portmanteau of formaldehyde and aldose. The reaction is catalyzed by a base and a divalent metal such as calcium.

The formose reaction was discovered in 1891and, providing it has a continuous supply of formaldehyde will continue to build larger molecules. The problem is, when the supply of formaldehyde runs out, the products of the reaction break down into a sort of tar of sugars. The reaction is also 'unselective' in that it produces a range of chemicals, few of which would have been useful to proto-cells.

What Quoc Phuong Tran's team found was that by adding, a small quantity of cyanamide to the reaction, some of the products can make ribonucleotides, effectively syphoning them off from the reaction. The output quantity is small, but the molecules are stable and less prone to breaking down when the reaction stops.

Quoc Phuong Tran and his colleagues published their findings in the journal *Chemical Science* (34). Tran also published an account of their work in *The Conversation* (35).

A common objection by creationists is that there is a classic 'chicken and egg' situation in the suggested mechanisms for abiogenesis in that at some point DNA became necessary for the synthesis of protein enzymes but proteins enzymes need DNA to carry the instructions for making them. What creationists presumably envisage is a magic deity setting up the system complete with all its 'irreducibly complex' parts.

However, this is based on the notion that the system couldn't have evolved from earlier systems in which DNA played no part until an enzyme capable of performing the function of reverse transcriptase to make DNA from an RNA template in the same way the retroviruses do.

In April of this year a research team led by Professor Koji Tamura, based at Tokyo University, Japan, showed that RNA structures known as ribozymes can carry out the function of proteins catalysts (enzymes) by catalysing key reactions. (36)

The discovery of ribozymes lends weight to the RNA World hypothesis where RNA served dual functions of "genetic information storage" and "catalysis," facilitating primitive life activities solely by RNA. While modern ribosomes are a complex of RNAs and proteins, ribozymes during early evolutionary stages may have been pieced together through the assembly of individual functional RNA units.

So, we also have an explanation for the origin of the ribosome where an RNA template is read to build the sequence of amino acids for the protein being coded for,

The team also found that when ATP is bound to the ribozyme it enhances its ability to join amino acids together by stabilizing the shape of the active site.

So, here we have a clear evolutionary pathway towards 'RNA world'.

In a paper which preceded the previous one by a month, three researchers at the Salk Institute for Biological Studies, La Jolla, California, USA (37), showed how a self-replicating system based on RNA could have bootstrapped from simple, self-catalysing lengths of RNA which not only self-replicate but can continue to do so even when there are variations stemming from faulty replications. This system would have created the variation needed for Darwinian evolution by natural selection as some variant performed better in terms of competing for resources and ultimately making more copies, so coming to predominate in the pool of RNA-based organisms.

This shows how Darwinian evolution by natural selection could have been partly responsible for producing the first fully-functional cells from primitive proto-cells, even before there was DNA and genes as we know them.

The concept of RNA world shouldn't come as news to creationist cult leaders since the idea has been around since

1960 when it was first proposed by scientists including Leslie Orgel, a fellow of the Salk Institute. Now the idea has been given renewed impetus by David Horning, Gerald Joyce, and Nikolaos Papastavrou. They have discovered an RNA enzyme that can make accurate copies of other functional RNA strands, while also allowing new variants of the molecule to emerge over time. These remarkable capabilities suggest the earliest forms of evolution may have occurred on a molecular scale in RNA.

The team were able to replicate the evolutionary process in the laboratory in respect of a ribozyme known as the 'hammerhead'. In these experiments, the researchers found that not only did the RNA polymerase ribozyme accurately replicate functional hammerheads, but over time, new variations of the hammerheads began to emerge. These new variants performed similarly, but their mutations made them easier to replicate, which increased their evolutionary fitness and led them to eventually dominate the lab's hammerhead population.

Briefly a little information about 'hammerheads' from ChatGPT3.5:

> The hammerhead ribozyme is a small catalytic RNA molecule that cleaves other RNA molecules in a sequence-specific manner. It is one of the best-characterized ribozymes and has been extensively studied in the field of RNA biochemistry and molecular biology. It gets its name from its secondary structure, which resembles the head of a hammer.
>
> It consists of three helical regions connected by loops, with a conserved catalytic core formed by conserved sequences within the loops. This core region contains the catalytic residues responsible for RNA cleavage. It functions by binding to a target RNA molecule through Watson-Crick base pairing interactions with

its substrate-binding arms. Once bound, the ribozyme catalyses the cleavage of the target RNA at a specific site, typically a purine-pyrimidine dinucleotide sequence.

The discovery and study of hammerhead ribozymes have contributed significantly to our understanding of RNA catalysis and have potential applications in biotechnology and gene therapy. Researchers have engineered hammerhead ribozymes for various purposes, including the specific cleavage of target RNA molecules for gene silencing or as tools for studying RNA structure and function.

In their statement of significance, the authors of the paper explain:

> An RNA enzyme with RNA polymerase activity was used to replicate and evolve an RNA enzyme with RNA-cleavage activity. The fidelity of the polymerase is sufficient to maintain heritable information over the course of evolution, with a succession of variants of the RNA-cleaving RNA enzyme arising that have progressively increased fitness. The RNA-catalyzed evolution of functional RNAs is thought to have been central to the early history of life on Earth and to the possibility of constructing RNA-based life in the laboratory.

Whether the first self-replicating, free-living proto-cells evolved around deep ocean thermal vents or on the surface in pool and on wet rocks, what they needed to get going was a supply of organic molecules, and a paper published in November 2024 in the journal *Astrobiology* by a team from Tohoku University, Tokyo University and Hokkaido University, Japan, led by Tatsuya Yoshida, showed how they could have been supplied in abundance.

The team succeeded in modelling the atmosphere of pre-biotic Earth. The atmosphere would have been composed of molecules of hydrogen (H_2) and methane (CH_4) and Earth was then rich in metallic iron (Fe) because there was little Oxygen to oxidise it., and importantly water vapour (H_2O).

According to the Tohoku University press release announcing this discovery:

> When exposed to solar ultraviolet (UV) radiation, these molecules undergo a chemical reaction that produces organics (also known as the "building blocks of life"). Part of these organics were precursors to essential biomolecules, such as amino acids and nucleic acids. However, understanding the role of UV radiation is difficult. Firstly, this type of atmosphere is unstable and likely underwent rapid changes due to atmospheric chemical reactions. Secondly, when UV radiation efficiently breaks down water vapour in the atmosphere and forms oxidative molecules, the precise branching ratio and timescale has not been determined. In order to address these issues, a 1D photochemical model was created to make accurate predictions about what the atmosphere was like on Earth long ago.
>
> The calculation reveals that most hydrogen was lost to space and that hydrocarbons like acetylene (produced from methane) shielded UV radiation. This inhibition of UV radiation significantly reduced the breakdown of water vapour and subsequent oxidation of methane, thus enhancing the production of organics. If the initial amount of methane was equivalent to that of the amount of carbon found on the present-day Earth's surface, organic layers several hundred metres thick could have formed.

So, by the action if UV radiation from the sun on the inorganic molecules in Earth's early atmosphere for a period of some 10-100 million years, the oceans could have accumulated the basic building blocks for organic organisms to get started, and all th result of chemistry and physics with no magic gods involved at any point.

And, as usual with scientific discoveries, the truth is shown to have little resemblance to the origin myths the parochial Bronze Age pastoralists made up to fill the yawning chasm in their knowledge and understanding of the world around them, with their belief that Earth had only existed for a few thousand years, so were blissfully ignorant of the 99.9975% of its history that occurred before then.

Origin of the Genetic Code

The last topic I'll deal with here is the origin of the genetic code where triplets in the four bases which form the backbone of DNA each code for a particular amino acid. I wrote about this in some details *Refuting Creationism: Why Creationism Fails in Both Its Science and Its Theology* (38) so I will be rather briefer here.

As is invariably the case, the objection of creationists to the idea that there could be a natural explanation to the origin of the genetic code is the same as their objections to a natural explanation for the Big Bang, abiogenesis, where 'life' comes from, consciousness, etc., is nothing more that ignorant incredulity and a notional assessment of probabilities based on nothing more substantial than guesswork. And their 'alternative' explanation is the usual presuppositional false dichotomy and god of the gaps fallacies, with never a scrap of evidence to show their preferred god exists and is capable of doing what they claim.

And, as usual, there is an explanation in which gods and magic have no role, so should have been pared away with

The Evidence from Science

Occam's Razor, apart from the fact that religious clerics and theologians need it to be included in the explanation.

The question, as with the 'fine-tuned Universe fallacy' is could the genetic code have been different? If it couldn't then the only question is, "How did it evolve?", not, "Why is it what it is?"

And the answer turns out to be that it very probably couldn't have been different. Remember, we are talking about a triplet code that originated in RNA, not DNA, because it was only later that RNA stored its information in the form of DNA, so the four bases we need to consider are cytosine (C), guanine, (G), adenine (A) and uracil (U). In DNA bases, uracil is replaced by thymine (T) otherwise the triplet code is the same.

Using 4 bases, the number of possible triplet combinations is 64 which is far more than the 20 or so amino acids in normal proteins and even allowing for some 'punctuation' like 'stop' there is considerable room for redundancy, and this is what we see in the third letter of the triplet code.

There is a strong link between the precursor from which the amino acid is synthesised and the first letter of the triplet. This correlation is so strong as to rule out pure chance.

So, is there a link between the second letter and something else pertinent to the amino acid it codes for? It turns out that there is indeed such a link – there is a close association between the second letter and the degree to which the amino acid is soluble or insoluble in wate . Amino acids can be sorted into a spectrum from very hydrophilic (water soluble) to very hydrophobic (fat soluble) and their position on this spectrum has a close association with the second letter in the triplet code. For example, five of the six most hydrophobic amino acids have T as the second letter in their triplet, the most hydrophilic all have A and the intermediates either C or G.

The Failure of Creationism

So this strongly suggests the code could have originated as a doublet code, but this code would have been error prone with a mutation in either letter changing the amino acid in the sequence, so the belief is that adding the third letter made the code more robust as a mutation has a one in three chance of being meaningless it simply changed the third letter. A doublet code also only codes for six different amino acids and, although that may have been enough for the earliest stages of RNA-based life, expanding it to a triplet code expanded the number of amino acids which could be incorporated into proteins.

Additionally, changes to the second letter would have substituted one amino acid for one with similar properties, so the function of the protein chain might not have been affected too seriously.

So, what all life on Earth has ended up with is a triplet genetic code that is fairly robust, but far from perfect – a near-enough-is-good-enough, utilitarian solution that we have come to expect of an evolved system working without a plan, and no intelligent input.

Although the first two letters if the triolet code would appear to have been inevitable, there was clearly a degree of freedom over the third letter, so it looks as though this code evolved in a proto-cell and proved so successful that it rapidly replaces all other possible evolving, self-replicating systems and so became 'frozen' as one of the fundamentals of living organisms that are so essential that they have been highly conserved throughout evolutionary history.

The last subject I will mention here applies specifically to Young Earth Creationism (YECism), and that is the impossibility of reconciling the belief in an Earth only 6-10,000 years old, which was the subject of a global genocidal flood about 4,000 years ago, with what archaeology, palaeontology, geology and cosmology reveal.

The Evidence from Science

It is difficult to tell from the propaganda produced by the Discovery Institute fellows in support of Intelligent design creationism to what extent they regard the account in genesis and the time-line of the Bible as literal history, or whether they only concern themselves with 'divine creation'.

Perhaps they are hedging their bets and, while they don't want to alienate real scientists on whose support they were banking by trying to argue for such absurd origine myths being literal truth, but don't want to alienate the Bible literalists and Evangelical Christians on whose financial support they depend. Certainly, Behe's books are widely cited by Young Earth Creationists (YECs) as are Dembski's and Tour's, but as always with YECs its probable that they haven't actually read the books but are simply parroting claims they heard but not understood.

I wrote about the Noah's Ark myth in *Refuting Creationism* so I won't dwell on it here, except to point out that such a flood would be expected to leave a global layer of silt covering mountains and valleys alike, full of the fossils of the animals and plants that would have been killed in the flood.

Since there would have been no barriers to how far this debris would drift, this inevitable layer of silt would contain the remains of plants and animals from disconnected land masses all jumbled together, with those of the dinosaurs YECs insist were alive at the time.

Needless to say, the predicted layer of silt is nowhere to be seen. Normally, the failure of a hypothesis to produce evidence for an inevitable consequence of it is sufficient to falsify the hypothesis and render it dead and buried as a scientific idea. But not so YECism, it seems. The absence of any supporting evidence is never a barrier to belief in something.

Another easily falsifiable prediction YECism makes is that there will be no geological, archaeological, palaeontologic or cosmological evidence older that when they believe the Universe was created in the legendary 'Creation Week'

The Geology, Archaeology and Palaeontology literature is full of research papers which, although the authors rarely set out to refute YECism, do so quite incidentally by showing how much at variance the facts are with what the Bible claims.

The Evidence from History

Historical evidence refutes YECism in particular because 99.9975% of Earth's history occurred before their supposed 'Creation Week' therefor anything which predates 6-10,000 years ago refutes the claim that there was no history prior to then.

As with the evidence from science, especially when the history is of biological system, there will be the inevitable evidence that the scientists are in no doubt at all that the Theory of Evolution provides the only scientific explanation for the observable facts. The childish notion of Intelligent design that creationist frauds keep assuring us is about to replace the TOE is making no inroads at all into mainstream science, for the simple reason that it is not science, explains nothing, make no useful predictions, and includes an unproven supernatural entity that has no place in science which should be pared away with Occam's Razor. Consciously or otherwise, that's exactly what professional scientists do.

Case 1. Humans Using Fire in Tasmania

I'll start with this paper because it was published as this book was in preparation.

It was published, open access, in the journal *Science Advances* (39) by a team of researchers from the UK and Australia, led by Dr Matthew Adeleye from Cambridge's Department of Geography, and shows, from an analysis of charcoal and pollen grains in mud, that the first inhabitants of Tasmania used fire to shape and manage the landscape.

This pushes the date for fire being used in Tasmania back by about 2,000 years and places it a full 31,600 years before creationists believe the Universe was created.

Modern Humans spread from Africa in the early part of the last Ice Ages and reached Northern Australia some 65,000 years ago. Tasmania currently lies about 240 kilometres off the southeast Australian coast, separated from the Australian mainland by the Bass Strait.

When the first Palawa/Pakana (Tasmanian Indigenous) communities eventually reached Tasmania (known to the Palawa people as Lutruwita), it was the furthest south humans had ever settled.

During the last Ice Age when water was locked up in the polar icecaps and glaciers, sea levers were lower than today, and Tasmania was connected to mainland Australia so the first people could walk there.

Analysis of the ancient mud taken from islands in the Bass Strait showed a sudden increase in charcoal around 41,600 years ago, followed by a major change in vegetation about 40,000 years ago, as indicated by different types of pollen in the mud.

The team used the services of two specialist laboratories, DirectAMS, Washington and Australian Nuclear Science and Technology Organization, Sydney, to discover the age of the charcoal by radiocarbon dating. Since I explained this method in some detail in *Refuting Creationism* I won't explain it all again, other than to say it is based on the fact that the radioactive isotope of carbon, ^{14}C (carbon-14) is produced in Earth's upper atmosphere by the action of solar radiation on nitrogen at a more or less constant rate. During a living organism's life, the carbon in its body, which comes from the food it eats contains a small proportion of ^{14}C along with the 'normal' carbon isotope ^{12}C.

When the plant or animal dies, no more carbon is incorporated into its body and the ^{14}C begins to decay to ^{12}C with a half-life of 5730 years. This means that after 5730 years half of the ^{14}C

will have decayed to the stable isotope of nitrogen, ^{14}N; in a further 5730 years half the remaining ^{14}C will have decayed.

The starting level of ^{14}C can be calibrated using dendrochronology – measuring the ^{14}C in wood of a known age (from tree-ring analysis) in the local area.

To ensure the ^{14}C measured is from the body of the plant or animals, the sample is carefully decontaminated to remove environmental sources of carbon which would distort the result. Finally, the analysis is carried out on several samples by two different laboratories and the results averaged, to give an estimated age plus or minus known variance. Because of the relatively short half-life of ^{14}C and the fact that the amount of ^{14}C gets smaller at time passed, this dating method is only accurate up to about 50,000 years.

Case 2. Change In Earth's Climate

In early November 2024, a team of scientists from Woods Hole Oceanographic Institution, the Lamont-Doherty Earth Observatory, the Scripps Institution of Oceanography, and Cardiff University, published date which shed light on an event that happened between 700,000 and 1,000,000 years ago when the large-scale patter of Earth's climate changed quite suddenly, in geological terms.

This event is known as the Mid-Pleistocene Transition (MPT) when the cycle of periods of glaciation interspersed with warmer period which repeated approximately every 41,000 years changed to one of about 100,000 years. The 41,000-year cycle was driven by sequential changes (precession) in the axis of Earth tilt about which it revolves, changing how much the poles were tilted away from the sun.

After the MPT, the cycle became much longer, and the temperature changes became more extreme. Something had changed and it wasn't the precession in the axis or rotation. What exactly that change was has been a matter of on-going scientific debate.

What the Woods Hole-led team have done is to analyse the microscopic fossils of organism known as foraminifera in seabed core samples taken from a site near South Africa, to measure the isotope of carbon, oxygen and neodymium in their bodies. The isotopes of carbon give a measure of the amount of atmospheric carbon dioxide (CO_2) compared to dissolved carbon in the seawater when they were alive. This is directly proportional to the CO_2 in the atmosphere.

The isotopes of oxygen show how cold the water was. This is possible because, die the difference in atomic weights between ^{18}O and ^{16}O, because in cold weather, ^{16}O evaporates more quickly and tends to get locked up in ice sheets, leaving the water richer in ^{18}O.

Lastly, neodymium isotopes act as water source tracers because the land the water in the sea flowed from has a characteristic molybdenum isotope signature.

From this date the team were able to build up a picture of changes in where the water came from, how cold it was and how much CO_2 there was in the atmosphere over the period of the MPT.

The team were able to rule out the hypothesis that the MPT was caused by changes in deep ocean currents, for which they found no evidence and concluded that it was caused by glacial ice sheets cooling the sea water and enabling it to hold more CO_2 in solution, so removing it from the atmosphere, casing temperatures to fall still further.

And this all happened 700,000 to 1,000,000 years ago when there were foraminifera to leave a record of the changes in their fossilised bodies.

Case 3. Grand Canyon at Rock Bottom

The Grand Canyon often features in creationist disinformation websites because it needs to be explained away in terms of a history of Earth lasting only some 6-10,000 years, and because it is easy to fool people who want to be fooled that it is somehow evidence if a global flood; in particular how the water in the alleged flood ran away. Cult frauds also pretend the different rock layers in the canyon wall can all be explained in terms of sediment deposited during their god's supposed genocidal flood.

The truth, as usual with creationist claims, is nothing like the childish myth they like to pretend is real history. In fact, the walls of the Grand Canyon are a record of plate tectonics and climate change over hundreds of millions of years and mesh completely with what is known of Earth's history from other sources.

An indication of how creationists cult leaders are terrified of the information in the walls of the Grand Canyon, can be gauged from the notorious creationist purveyor of disinformation, Dr. Andrew A. Snelling's article on the creationists' disinformation site, Answers in Genesis (40) and the lengths he went to to obtain sample without disclosing exactly where he got them from, as related in an article by Amanda Reilly in *Science* (41).

Snelling, who has described himself as a Christian missionary (43) argued that being required to provide GPS coordinates for his samples discriminated against him on religious grounds because other scientists had not been required to provide this information. Religious fanatics like nothing more than feeling they're being victimised! Clearly, Snelling believes his religion requires his 'science' to lack precision and reproducibility in case someone else tried to replicate his measurements and finds his to be bogus.

Snelling was subsequently given permission to collect samples under supervision and then wrote up his findings to try to explain away the fact that they didn't conform to his YEC preconceptions. His excuses include the creationists go-to excuse - the unsubstantiated claim that the uniformly old age of the rock he obtained must be because radioactive decay rates used to be different by several orders of magnitude!

One of Snellings stated objectives was to prove that the deformed Tapeats sandstone deposits, which he assures his readers are not fractured, despite the fact that photographs show fractures, were soft when deformed. He mentions this early in his article but then quietly drops the subject, presumably because his findings contradict his claim.

His findings are soundly refuted by James McKay in BioLogos (42).

Dr. Andrew A. Snelling, who contributes to creationist websites such as Answers in Genesis (AiG), arguing that the geological evidence supports the idea that Earth is a mere 6-10,000 years old and was subjected to a destructive global flood about 4,000 years ago, appears to be the same Dr. Andrew A Snelling who wrote the following in a standard reference work on the Koongarra Uranium Deposits in Australia's Northern Territory (Page 807-812) (43):

> "The Archaean[32] basement consists of domes of granitoids and granitic gneisses (the Nanambu Complex), the nearest outcrop being 5 km to the

---

[32] The Archaean (or Archean) eon is the geological period after the Hadean and before the Proterozoic. It is one of the four main time periods (eons) of Earth history. The Archaean lasted from 4,000 million years ago (mya) to 2,500 mya. It contains the first sedimentary rocks, and the first fossil life forms, which were cyanobacteria, and acritarchs.

north. Some of the lowermost overlying Proterozoic metasediments were accreted to these domes during amphibolite grade regional metamorphism (5 to 8 kb and 550° to 630° C) at 1870 to 1800 Myr[33]. Multiple isoclinal recumbent folding accompanied metamorphism."

Later in the same work, he writes:

"A 150 Myr period of weathering and erosion followed metamorphism."

Amongst other references to geological process and formations being hundreds of millions of years old, Snelling also say, in effect:

1. During Early Proterozoic times (from 1688-1600 million years ago) the area was covered by thick, flat-lying sandstones.
2. At some later date (but after the reverse faulting) the Koongarra uranium mineral deposit forms, perhaps in several stages, first between 1650-1550 million years ago, and later around 870 and 420 million years.
3. The last stage, the weathering of the primary ore to produce the secondary dispersion fan above the No 1 orebody seems to have begun only in the last 1-3 million years.

As a contributor to AiG, Snelling is required to sign an oath stating that he subscribes to its articles of faith that state the geological evidence is subservient to the belief that the account of creation *ex nihilo* in the Bible is definitive truth, so I'll leave the reader to assess the sincerity or otherwise of Dr. Anderw A Snelling's professed YECism.

For more on this see *Will the Real Dr. Snelling Please Stand Up* by Dr Alex Ritchie. (44)

---

[33] Million years

Clearly, the Grand Canyon is a source of embarrassment for YECs, but perhaps the most embarrassing feature for them is the famous horseshoe bend in which the rivers bed turns through over 180 degrees. Creationists are required to believe that a raging torrent of water reversed its direction of flow for no apparent reason.

And now we have a recent paper by a team from Utah State University, together with colleagues from the University of New Mexico, Boise State University, Idaho, the University of Las Vegas, Nevada and the Denver Museum of Nature & Science, Denver, Colorado, which shows. the rocks at the bottom of the canyon are from the Cambrian, 540 million years before creationists dogma says Earth was made from nothing by magic.

The team examined the Tonto Group of rocks from the Grand Canyon, looking for fossils that give a clue to their age.

The Tonto Group of rocks represents the earliest widespread marine sediments deposited on the North American craton during the Cambrian Explosion. It consists of:

Tapeats Sandstone, consisting of coarse-grained sandstone, conglomerate layers, and some interbedded shales. It was deposited in a shallow, advancing coastline or beach environment during a marine transgression. It is known for containing abundant ripple marks and cross-bedding, as well as pebbles and cobbles indicative of high-energy environments such as a beach with breaking waves. It sometimes contains traces of early marine life, such as trilobite tracks.

Bright Angel Shale. A greenish to reddish-brown shale with some interbedded sandstone and siltstone layers., formed in a quieter, offshore marine setting, such as tidal flats or shallow marine shelves. This deposit contains fossilized remains of Cambrian marine organisms like trilobites, brachiopods, and trace fossils of burrowing organisms.

Muav Limestone. A grey to buff limestone, sometimes dolomitic, with occasional interbedded siltstone and sandstone. It was deposited in a deeper marine environment as the sea transgressed further inland. It contains fossilized marine life like trilobites, brachiopods, and algae is more abundant here, indicating a fully marine ecosystem.

The Tonto Group records the "Great Cambrian Transgression", when rising sea levels flooded the continents, forming widespread shallow seas. This transgression is captured in the Tonto Platform, a prominent, relatively flat erosional feature in the Grand Canyon.

Geologically, these layers demonstrate the principle of superposition (younger layers on top of older ones) and offer evidence of changing environments over time. Together, they illustrate the Sauk Sequence, a major North American stratigraphic feature reflecting marine inundation during the Cambrian. (Information on the Tonto Group supplied by ChatGPT4o)

The team, led by Professor Carol Dehler, of the Department of Geosciences, Utah State University were reassessing the Edwin Dinwiddie McKee's[34] studies in the late 1960 and early 1970s in which he proposes a single inundation in the Cambrian as sea levels rose. What the team found was that there had been not one but five separate inundations as sea levels rose and fell. They have published their findings in the journal of The Geological Society of America, *GSA Today*. (45)

---

[34] Edwin Dinwiddie McKee (1906–1984) was an influential American geologist, palaeontologist, and sedimentologist, best known for his pioneering studies of the Grand Canyon's geology. (ChatGPT4o)

Case 4. The Origin of Domestic Cattle

Creationists of all flavours believe all animals were created in a special act of creation and Bible-literalist creationists believe they were all created for the benefit of humans because the Bible relates the myth of God creating all the animals as an 'help meet' for Adam who then named them. For the creations of an omniscient designer, these were a signal failure as Adam didn't select any of them, so, in the second version of the creation myth, God then created Eve as a clone of Adam (Genesis 2: 19-22)

From that, creationists conclude that all species on earth are there for humans. The slight problem with that is that these don't seem to have been fit for purpose either as almost without exception, our domestic animals have been improved so much so that the wild forms are sometime almost unrecognisable as the same species.

Another problem is that many species live in environments that are hostile to humans so were unknown to us until we had the technology to discover them. Many of these extremophiles live in the ocean abyss, around thermal vents in mid-ocean ridges for example. If someone can suggest a use for the giant tube worms which don't have a digestive tract but live off the sulphur-eating bacteria that live symbiotically in the tube worms, then I'd be grateful to learn of it, and how we managed without them until they were discovered a few years ago.

But that's by the bye; the subject here is the domestication of modern domestic cattle, *Bos taurus*, the ancestors of which were widely depicted in cave painting in southern France and Northern Spain – the auroch, *Bos primigenius*. The last Aurochs roamed Europe and Asia from about 650,000 years ago. The last recorded wild aurochs became extinct in 1627 due to hunting, habitat destruction and diseases spread by domestic cattle.

The Evidence from History

The auroch was a large and dangerous beast which Julius Caesar described as 'like an elephant'. Although he was exaggerating, an auroch bull stood about 6 feet tall at the shoulder and weighing up to 1,500 pounds; the cows were a little smaller but dangerous none-the-less. This probably explains why a team investigating the origins of domestic cattle found they are descended from a very small number of wild aurochs and all share the same few female ancestors, as shown by their mitochondrial DNA. Evidently an auroch docile enough to be domesticated was a rarity.

They have published their findings in *Nature* (46)

By examining DNA recovered from 38 auroch remains stretching back over 50,000 years – from 40,000 years before creationists think Earth and the animals on it were created - the team have shown that as the last Ice Age progressed, aurochs were split into at least three populations or sub-species with very little interbreeding, like a species undergoing allopatric speciation. They remained isolated until the glaciers retreated, when they could mix and interbreed again.

These populations were in Western Europe, Italy and the Balkans and each population contributed genes to the domestic cattle, but the first domestic cattle were from so few individuals that they effectively went through a very narrow genetic bottleneck. However, as they spread east and west, there were further ingressions of auroch genes due to wild bulls mating with domestic cows, giving us the wide variety of selectively bred cattle that we see today.

As an act of creation, the auroch, if it was intended to be Man's 'helpmeet' as a provider of meat and dairy products, was almost a disaster. Had not a small number of them been docile enough to be domesticated, maybe by rearing orphaned calves, there would be no domestic cattle. Instead, it would have been just another example of extinct Eurasia megafauna as modern humans spread.

Case 5. Archaic Hominins Butchering Elephants

By insisting that everything that has ever happened on Earth must have happened in the last 6-10,000 years, creationists manage to exclude some 99.9975% of Earth's rich history, so not surprisingly, nearly every archaeological and paleoecological discovery refutes their claim,

An example of this was the discovery published in the *Journal of Vertebrate Paleontology* in August 2024 (47), that the remains of extinct elephants, *Palaeoloxodon turkmenicus* excavated from a site in India showed unmistakeable signs of having been butchered with stone tools to remove the meat from the bones. The stone tools are made of basalt, a stone not found nearby, so they must have been carried to the site for the purpose to which they were put.

The site is at Pampore in the Kashmir Valley, and it seems soon after the elephants were butchered the river flooded and covered the site with silt, burying a number of stone tools with the remains. The team who carried out the excavation, included Advait Jukar, a curator of vertebrate palaeontology at the Florida Museum of Natural History.

Since anatomically modern humans did not leave Africa before about 50-60,000 years ago, the beings who made the stone tools and did the butchering must have been the descendants of *Homo erectus*, who migrated into Eurasia much earlier. This raised the possibility that they could have been Denisovans who are believed to have spread across East and Southeast Asia.

To date, only one fossil hominin — the Narmada human — has ever been found on the Indian subcontinent, in 1982. Its mix of features from older and more recent hominin species indicate the Indian subcontinent must have played an important role in early human dispersal.

As well as the evidence of human butchery (we don't know how the elephants died) the remains are scientifically interesting for another reason. Fossils of this extinct species, which was almost twice the size of modern elephants, *Loxodonta africana.* They are also rare, only one set having previously been discovered. *P. turkmenicus* is thought to have become extinct toward the end of the Pleistocene, around the same time as many other large mammals. Climate change, habitat changes, and potentially human activity may have contributed to its decline.

The *Palaeoloxodon* (old elephants) genus originated in Africa and, like the Hominins, migrated into Eurasia. There it diversified into the European straight-tusked elephant, *P. antiquus* and *P. turkmenicus.* In Africa, the genus evolved into the African bush elephant, *Loxodonta africana*, and the African forest elephant, *L. cyclotis.*

Again, like humans, there is evidence of interbreeding as the ancestral species diversified and spread. For example, *P. antiquus* probably had an ingression if genes from both *L. cycotis* and the stem species that later diversified into the Woolly mammoth, *Mammuthus premogenius* and the Columbian mammoth, *Mammuthus colunbi*, shortly after that stem species split from the Asian elephant, *Elephas maximus*.

No evidence there of special creation followed by extinction, which begs the question, why would an intelligent designer design so many megafaunas to go extinct and give them genomes which made it look like they had evolved from a common ancestor which diverged into different species that sometimes interbreed?

Case 6. Humans Spread Across Europe

Creationists are handicapped by trying to compress the entire 13.8 billion year history of the Universe, the 3.8 billion year history of planet Earth and the 2-3 million year history of human evolution, into 10,000 or fewer years, and then trying to ignore the evidence of continuous, unbroken cultural history extending from way before a supposed global genocidal flood 4,000 years ago, right through it and continuing to modern times, as though no such a flood ever happened.

For example, we now have evidence of how early modern human migrated across Europe during the Aurignacian[35] (43,000 -32,000 years ago).

The Aurignacian period is associated with the arrival and expansion of anatomically modern humans in Europe. These humans are believed to have migrated from Africa, bringing with them new technologies, cultural practices, and survival strategies.

The period overlaps with the gradual disappearance of Neanderthals, who had previously inhabited Europe. It is believed there was some cultural exchange between Neanderthals and modern humans during this time and they appear to have interbred at least occasionally. One school of thought is that Neanderthals may not have been exterminated by modern humans but were simply absorbed into the much larger and growing *H. sapiens* population. Non-African people now have 1-3% Neanderthal genes so there is more Neanderthal DNA in the world than there ever were before the entry of modern humans into Eurasia.

---

[35] The Aurignacian is an archaeological industry of the Upper Palaeolithic associated with Early European modern humans (EEMH) lasting from 43,000 to 26,000 years ago.

The Evidence from History

The research comes from a team from the University of Cologne, Germany, led by Professor Dr Yaping Shao, who published their findings, open access, in Nature Communications (48).

The team developed a mathematical model, the human existence potential (HEP) which was derived from three components:

- φ_E for 'Environment' that was conducive to human habitation given the level of technological development of the time?
- φ_{Ac} for Accessibility - how accessible were the resources with that technology?
- φ_{Av} for Availability - what resources were available?

This brought together experts in Geophysics, Meteorology and Palaeoarchaeology.

The model reveals four phases of the process:

1. A slow expansion of human settlement from the Eastern Mediterranean coast to the Balkans.
2. A rapid expansion into western Europe.
3. A decline in human population.
4. A regional increases in population density and further advances into previously unsettled areas of Great Britain and the Iberian Peninsula.

The underlying driver of these phases was a combination of climate and advances in technology, social structures and culture. And it all happened between 33 and 26 thousand years before creationists believe Earth was created and moreover the archaeological remains which record these changes are still there to be discovered with no hint of the predictable layer of silt that a global genocidal flood 4000 years ago would have deposited on them, if it hadn't swept them away completely. The beautiful cave paintings, which would have been destroyed, are still there too.

Case 7. Co-Evolution of Humans and Sled Dogs

Around the time Creationism's god was busy, according to their favourite mythology, creating a small flat planet with a dome over it, somewhere in the Middle East, unbeknown to the authors of the myth, there were people living in Siberia, Alaska and Northern Canada.

A land bridge known as Beringia, which was there when sea levels were lower during a period of maximum glaciation, had enabled these people to migrate into North America from Siberia, and there, people were forming a symbiotic evolutionary relationship with a domesticated Siberian wolf.

 By selectively breeding from the strongest and with the greatest stamina. They were selectively breeding them to create a breed of cold-tolerant dog capable of great feats of endurance and, as aa part of a team, able to pull a loaded sled at a steady run for many miles and survive outdoors in the harshest of Arctic weather.

As with all the other domesticated animals which creationist legend says were created especially for humans, they needed to be considerably altered by selective breeding to make them fit for purpose. Apparently, creationism's god didn't know what we would use them for or how to design them for that purpose and had to leave it up to us.

Now a little bit of that human-dog coevolution has been clarified somewhat by researchers investigating the origins of the Arctic sled dogs. The results of their research, led by Professor Heather Jay Huson of Cornell University, Ithaca, NY, is published open access in the Oxford Academic journal *Genome Biology and Evolution* (49).

Their massive genomic survey of the Siberian husky has revealed that sled dogs descended from two distinct lineages of Arctic canids and originated in the northeastern Siberian Arctic, generations earlier than previously thought. The study also showed that approximately half of all Siberian huskies bred for racing have introgression with European breeds.

If only the authors of the Hebrew origin myths, that creationists think are real history, had had the slightest inkling that there were people domesticating dogs to work in Arctic conditions in Siberia and North America, they could have written a slightly more plausible mythology. As it was, they wrote about the only place and time they knew – the Middle East in the late Bronze Age - so there is nothing in the mythology that wasn't within a couple of days walk from their pastures in the Canaanite Hills.

Case 8. Two of Our Elephants Are Missing

Any children's toy Noah's Ark wouldn't be complete without a pair of elephants, a couple of zebras and maybe a pair each of ostriches and rhinos, and yet none of those animals is mentioned in the Bible which causes a problem for creationists trying to force-fit extant species into the Bible's list of 'kinds'. If, like the Bible's authors, you define birds as 'flying kinds' which includes bats, where do ostriches go? Are they not bird 'kind'?

The simple reason for these glaring omissions in the Bible is that the authors didn't know about them. There are no elephants in the Bible. For that matter, there is no mention of anywhere or anything outside a small area of the Middle East during the Bronze Age, which gives a clue as to where and when it was written.

It also gives a clue as to the level of ignorance of the authors – not something that would apply if it had been written by an omniscient creator god as was later decreed to be the case after several disparate books that were never intended to be bound up together and forced into an unlikely narrative were gathered up and called God's Holy Word.

Not only are most extant animals, even big ones you couldn't miss if you went to where they lived, not in the Bible but nor are any extinct species. There are none of the now-extinct megafauna of Eurasia such as mammoths, aurochs, Steppe bison and woolly rhinos and there is definitely no mention of continents such as North and South America, Antarctica or Australia and no southern hemisphere at all.

And of course there are no large islands such as Madagascar, Great Britain, Greenland, New Guinea or Vancouver in the Bible because the authors didn't know about them either, they couldn't possibly have been aware that there were mammoths living on the island of Vancouver between 13,000 years and at least 35,000 years before they set their creation myth to try to fill the gaps in their knowledge and understanding with narratives that made sense within their narrow framework of understanding. That framework included magic but no appreciation of the history or geography of the planet or of life on it. What a story they could have invented if only they had had more than childish guesswork to go with!

How we know there were mammoths on Vancouver Island all those years ago to a time well before creationists believe Earth was created, is due to the work of Dr. Laura Termes, PhD and colleagues, from Simon Fraser University, who examined 32 suspected mammoth samples collected on Vancouver Island.

Of those samples, just 16 were considered suitable for radiocarbon dating.

The youngest sample was found to be around 23,000 years old and the oldest turned out to be beyond the range radiocarbon dating could measure, meaning it was older than 45,000 years.

Prior to the study, only two mammoth remains found on Vancouver Island had ever been dated. Both lived around 21,000 years ago, so the Termes' study provides a greater understanding of when the massive mammals lived in the area. The Team published their findings in the *Canadian Journal of Earth Sciences.* (50)

Case 9. The Neanderthals of the Pyrenees

The Abric Pizarro is an archaeological site located in the Pyrenean foothills of southwestern France. This site has gained significant attention for its well-preserved evidence of Neanderthal habitation, particularly during the Middle Palaeolithic period, between roughly 100,000 and 65,000 years ago. The site provides crucial insights into the lives of the Neanderthals who occupied this region.

The Abric Pizarro site is a rock shelter situated within a broader landscape that would have been rich in resources for the Neanderthals. The Pyrenean foothills were a diverse environment with access to water, varied vegetation, and an abundance of game. This location would have been ideal for the seasonal movement of hunter-gatherer groups, providing shelter from the elements and proximity to essential resources.

The archaeological evidence at Abric Pizarro indicates that Neanderthals used this site repeatedly over thousands of years. The layers of sediment found in the rock shelter contain numerous artifacts, including stone tools, animal bones, and other material remains that suggest a range of activities took place here.

The stone tools recovered from Abric Pizarro are characteristic of the Mousterian tradition, which is associated with Neanderthals across Europe. They were made primarily from locally available stone and include hand axes, scrapers, and points. They were used for various purposes, including hunting, butchering animals, and processing plant material

The animal remains discovered at the site provide evidence that the Neanderthal diet was heavily reliant on large game such as deer, horses, and possibly even smaller mammals. The presence of cut marks on bones suggests that the Neanderthals at Abric Pizarro were proficient hunters and that they butchered animals on-site for food.

Some researchers believe that the site was likely used seasonally, with Neanderthals returning to the shelter at certain times of the year when game was more plentiful or when the weather made other areas less hospitable. This seasonal occupation would have been part of a typical nomadic pattern of movement across the landscape, as Neanderthal adapted to changing environments over time.

Now a team of archaeologists has shown that the Neanderthals who used the rock shelter were skilled hunters who were able to adapt to changing conditions, and far from the slow-witted, lumbering creatures of popular mythology.

The Australian National University and Autonomous University of Barcelona team, led by Dr. Sofia C. Samper Carro, have just published their findings in the *Journal of Archaeological Science*.

Dr Samper said, "The unique site at Abric Pizarro gives a glimpse of Neanderthal behaviour in a landscape they had been roaming for hundreds of thousands of years. Neanderthals disappeared around 40,000 years ago. Suddenly,

The Evidence from History

we modern humans appear in this region of the Pyrenees, and the Neanderthals disappear. But before that, Neanderthals had been living in Europe for almost 300,000 years. They clearly knew what they were doing. They knew the area and how to survive for a long time.

"This is one of the most interesting things about this site, to have this unique information about when Neanderthals were alone and living in harsh conditions and how they thrived before modern humans appeared."

Using a variety of dating techniques, the team were able to show the site was occupied during what is known in geology as the MS4 period. This is a period of extensive glaciation when Earth entered a cold spell due probably to the Milankovitch cycles[36]. The MS4 period, also called the MIS4 period stands for 'Marine Isotope Sediment Stage 4'. It is based on analysing the isotopes of oxygen in the fossilized bodies of foraminifera that I mentioned earlier.

Briefly, oxygen exists as two stable isotopes, ^{16}O and ^{18}O and being slightly lighter, water (H_2O) with ^{16}O evaporates more quickly that that with heavier isotope. This lighter water then gets locked up in the ice sheets, so the more extensive the ice sheets are, the more ^{16}O is removed from sea water and the relative ratio of ^{18}O increases.

The fossilised bodies of foraminifera record this changing ratio ($\delta^{18}O$) in their shells so by analysing these micro-fossils

---

[36] Milankovitch cycles describe the collective effects of changes in the Earth's movements on its climate over thousands of years. The term was coined and named after the Serbian geophysicist and astronomer Milutin Milanković. In the 1920s, he hypothesized that variations in eccentricity, axial tilt, and precession combined to result in cyclical variations in the intra-annual and latitudinal distribution of solar radiation at the Earth's surface, and that this orbital forcing strongly influenced the Earth's climatic patterns. (Wikipedia)

in marine sediment, geologists can tell how the temperature of sea water changed over time.

Interestingly, from the point of view of creationists intent on disputing this dating method, the scientist got similar results when the used chronometric dating methods on artifacts recovered from Abric Pizarro. These included optically stimulated luminescence (OSL) and thermoluminescence dating.

I explained these in *Refuting Creationism* (38) but briefly, OSL, which would have been used for dating stone tools, for example, depends on the fact that, minerals are continually subject to background radiation from the decay of radioactive isotopes in their environment. This causes electrons to become trapped in the crystal matrix. Exposure to solar radiation then releases these electrons. However, if the artifacts become buried and shielded from sunlight, they continue to accumulate trapped electrons.

When subjected to heat or intense light, these electrons will then be released and can be detected using sensitive equipment. The age since the artifact was buried is proportional to the quantity of electrons accumulated.

Creationists who depend on the claim that radioactive decay rates have changed by several orders of magnitude in the last 6-10,000 years (an irrational belief that would mean atoms could not have existed and the sea would have boiled away when their creator god supposedly created life on a planet perfect for it to exist on) will be distressed to learn that both the analysis of fossilised foraminifera and OSL dating gave consistent results, yet .radioactive decay has nothing to do with $\delta^{18}O$ dating!

So, here we have solid evidence that an archaic hominin was alive and well in Northern Spain between 90,000 and 50,000 years before creationists believe there was an Earth for them to live on.

Case 10. Mass Migration of Farmers into Iberia

The reason we have the Ancient Hebrew origins myths that make up the first five books of the Bible is an accident of history. They happened to be from a part of the world that was later Hellenised with its well-established writing, so the myths could be recorded (which effectively fossilises an oral tradition). That part of the world was then inherited from the Greeks by their Roman successors and the rest is history.

Had that been true of other parts of the world, such as Central Asia or the Iberian Peninsula, for example, our cultural influence and record of history. Would have been different and might have born more resemblance to what actually happened.

And what actually happened utterly refutes the ancient Hebrew mythology, especially its time-line which appear to start only 6-10,000 years ago, with a genocidal flood about 4,000 years ago, if you read it literally.

But that can't possibly be true, because we now know that around 4,200 years ago when, according to the Hebrew mythology, Earth was under 29,000 feet of water, people known as the Yamnaya, a Bronze Age farming culture, were migrating from the Pontic-Caspian steppe region (modern-day Ukraine and southern Russia) into the Iberian Peninsula where they replaced an earlier population of neolithic modern humans.

The stimulus for this migration was probably a search for more grazing land for animal stocks and a growing population. The Yamnaya culture, often considered a key representative of the steppe pastoralist lifestyle, originated in the Pontic-Caspian steppe[37] around 5,000–4,500 years ago.

---

[37] The Pontic–Caspian Steppe is a steppe extending across Eastern

They were highly mobile, pastoralists (herding sheep, cattle, and horses), and are believed to have used wheeled vehicles like carts and wagons.

Genetic and archaeological evidence suggests that groups of Yamnaya or their descendants began migrating westward into Europe around 4,500 to 4,300 years ago, reaching as far as Central and Western Europe. It is thought they brought the Indo-European language to Europe, from which almost all modern European, Iranian and Northen Indian languages have evolved.

Before the arrival of these migrants, the languages spoken in Iberia were pre-Indo-European, now the only remnant of those is Euskara (Basque).

It is about this time that DNA analysis of human remains in Iberia shows a distinctive Y-chromosome, R1b, a signature marker of the Central Asian Yamnaya people, became the predominant male haplotype in Iberia.

There was also a change from the communal burials of the Copper Age to the single and double tombs of the Bronze Age El Argar society.

Some have interpreted this to indicate the invasion of Iberia by the Yamnaya was a violent conquest, but there are other interpretations such as cultural dominance and maybe enslavement of indigenous women.

Now new research, by a group of archaeologists from the Universitat Autònoma de Barcelona (UAB) and Universidad de Murcia, Spain has shed more light on this question. The

---

Europe to Central Asia, formed by the Caspian and Pontic steppes. It stretches from the northern shores of the Black Sea (the *Pontus Euxinus* of antiquity) to the northern area around the Caspian Sea, where it ends at the Ural-Caspian narrowing, which joins it with the Kazakh Steppe in Central Asia, making it a part of the larger Eurasian Steppe. (Wikipedia).

team looked at a large sample of radiocarbon (^{14}C) dates from human bones discovered in these different types of graves.

This has shown that the change from communal burials was sudden and also shows that there was a peak of burials between 2550 and 2400 BCE, followed by a sudden drop in 2300-2250 BCE.

These figures suggest that there may have been a rapid decline in the population of Iberia for reasons unknown, so what the invaders found was a small population that was easily absorbed into the growing Yamnaya population rather than the wholesale violent replacement of the indigenous population by invaders.

And all these interesting developments in early European history were occurring during the time the inventors of the Bible mythology were placing their genocidal global flood which would had obliterated the remains the research team analysed to arrive at their results when rather than the human population being reduced to a mere eight, there was a large-scale migration of farming people bringing new technology, a new language, a new culture and new DNA into Western Europe.

Case 11. The Mass Extinction that Killed the Dinosaurs

If there is anything guaranteed to have creationists metaphorically, if not actually, screwing up their eyes, putting their hands over their ears and jumping up and down shouting "'Tisn't! 'Tisn't! 'Tisn't!" its news about the mass extinction 66 million years before 'Creation Week' that exterminated all but the non-avian dinosaurs and the early mammals and about 75% of all other species.

This event reminds them not only that Earth is very much older that their cult requires them to believe but also that Earth is not the 'finely-tuned' haven for life that their belief in a perfect creator requires them to believe. Instead, Earth is very old and subject to unpredictable catastrophes, not the least of which are cosmological events such as meteor strikes and the consequential mass extinctions.

Now a team of geoscientists from the University of Cologne have led an international study to determine the origin of the huge piece of rock that hit the Earth around 66 million years ago and permanently changed the climate. They have discovered that the meteor was unusual in that it came from a region of space outside the orbit of Jupiter. They recently published their findings in the journal *Science* (51).

According to a widely accepted theory, the mass extinction at the Cretaceous-Paleogene boundary was triggered by the impact of an asteroid at least 10 kilometres in diameter near Chicxulub on the Yucatán Peninsula in Mexico. The asteroid, together with a large quantities of earth rock vaporized, spreading dust particles into the stratosphere and obscured the sun. This led to dramatic changes in the living conditions on the planet and severely restricted photosynthetic activity for several years.

The dust particle eventually settled out to leave a thin, global layer of sediment containing a high level of platinum-group metals (iridium, ruthenium, osmium, rhodium, platinum, and palladium), which come from the asteroid and are otherwise extremely rare in the rock that forms the Earth's crust. By analysing the isotopic composition ruthenium in this layer, the scientists discovered that the asteroid originally came from the outer solar system.

By analysing the ruthenium isotope compositions for other craters and impact structures of different ages on Earth the scientists showed that within the last 500 million years, well over 80 percent of all asteroid fragments that hit the Earth, originated from the inner solar system, in contrast to the impact at the Cretaceous-Paleogene boundary.

What will upset creationists is not only that this occurred so long before their legendary 'Creation Week', but also the fact that this impact left a global layer as a record, whereas their favourite global catastrophe, the legendary genocidal flood just a few thousand years ago, left no such trace. Not even a fossil from the wrong landmass of even a collection of sediment in an alpine valley consistent with being deposited there during a period of submergence beneath thousands of feet of water, containing the bodies of millions of drowned animals and plant debris.

Case 11. How The Milky Way Was Formed.

The final case in this series is what astronomers have discovered concerning the formation of the Milky Way. Of course, there is no room or need for magic deities speaking magic words to make it all pop up out of nothing, like the bronze Age pastoralist though it might have been done. Instead, what we have is the operation of the basic laws of physics acting over vast distances and times on a scale the Bronze Age authors of the Bible could only have guessed at.

First, we need to deal with the idea that looking further into space is also looking further back in time because we are sing objects as they were when the light out instruments detect left them. If these objects are, say, 12 billion light years away, what we see is the Universe as it was 12 billion years ago because it has taken the light that long to reach us. This means, in theory, if we could look far enough into space, we would see the Big Bang. Unfortunately, for the first 300,000 years the Universe was opaque because atoms had not formed and photons couldn't pass through the charged electromagnetic fields, so that acts as a barrier beyond which we can never see.

So, how do astronomers know what the Universe was like when the Milky Way was formed? They can see it, of course, and no matter how far or in which direction they look they never see a small flat planet with a dome over it as described in Genesis. Instead, they see hundreds of billions of galaxies each with hundreds of billions of stars, many of which are now known to have planets orbiting round them. To paraphrase the semi-literate Donald Trump, we live on a planet in a bigly galaxy in an even biglier Universe.

How do astronomers know how far away bodies are in space? The answer is the 'red shift'. The more the light coming from a body is red shifted, the further away it is. This phenomenon is cause by the Universe expanding so light travelling through space as it increases gets stretched out and the longer wavelengths are at the red end of the visible light spectrum.

There is a subtle distinction here between the Doppler effect which is cause by a body moving relative to the observer, and the cosmological red shift which is caused by the space between the observer and the object increasing, so the red shift is the same wherever the observer is in space, unlike the Doppler effect which would only be the same everywhere for an observer at the center of the Universe.

And, thanks to the work of two scientists working at the Max Planck Institute for Astronomy, Heidelberg, Germany, we now know our galaxy, the Milky Way galaxy was formed by the merger of two smaller galaxies. The scientists, Khyati Malhan and Hans-Walter Rix combined date from the European Space Agency's (ESA) astrometry satellite Gaia and the Sloan Digital Sky Survey[38] (SDSS) survey. Their findings are published in *The Astrophysical Journal* (52).

---

[38] The Sloan Digital Sky Survey or SDSS is a major multi-spectral imaging and spectroscopic redshift survey using a dedicated 2.5-m

The Evidence from History

That there were two original galaxies that merged comes from the fact that as they merge, stars within the merging galaxies will retain their original angular momentum, so, with a large enough and accurate enough data set which records the movement of stars over time, scientists can estimate which stars originated in which galaxy.

So, going to the heart of YEC beliefs about a universe with a small flat planet with a dome over it, magically made from nothing, as the Bible literally describes, we now know the Milky Way galaxy in which our star exists was itself created without magic 13-14 billion years ago out of two proto galaxies.

Amusingly, the two astronomers chose to name the two proto-galaxies after Hindu deities Shiva and Shakti.

It might come as a surprise to fundamentalist Christians but there are other religions with equally fanciful, evidence-free superstitions that believers believe explain the universe. I'll briefly outline the Hindu tradition here, not as an alternative science but as an alternative religious view of the universe and our place in it.

What objective evidence is there to distinguish between one and the other?

In the Hindu mythology, these deities are fundamental aspects of the divine:

Shiva is one of the principal deities of Hinduism. He is often referred to as the destroyer within the Trimurti, the Hindu trinity that includes Brahma (the creator) and Vishnu (the preserver). Shiva is also known as the god of meditation, yoga, and arts. He is usually depicted as a yogi, adorned with

---

wide-angle optical telescope at Apache Point Observatory in New Mexico, United States. The project began in 2000 and was named after the Alfred P. Sloan Foundation, which contributed significant funding.

snakes and a crescent moon on his head, with a third eye on his forehead representing wisdom and insight. Shiva is often associated with asceticism, but he's also a family man, as he's married to the goddess Parvati and has two sons, Ganesha and Kartikeya.

Shakti is the divine feminine energy and the primordial cosmic power in Hinduism. She is the personification of the creative energy of the Universe. Shakti is often depicted as a goddess, sometimes alongside Shiva, and sometimes as an independent deity. She represents the dynamic forces that move through the entire cosmos. Shakti is considered the mother goddess, the source of all, and is revered in various forms such as Durga, Kali, Parvati, and others.

The concepts of Shiva and Shakti are prominently featured in various Hindu scriptures and holy texts. Some of the key texts where these ideas are explored include:

1. The Vedas are the oldest and most authoritative scriptures of Hinduism. While they don't directly mention Shiva and Shakti as distinct deities, the concepts they embody are foundational to later Hindu philosophy and theology.

2. The Puranas are a genre of ancient Hindu texts that provide detailed narratives about various deities, cosmology, and religious practices. Shiva and Shakti are prominently featured in several Puranas, including the Shiva Purana, Devi Bhagavata Purana, and Devi Mahatmya (part of Markandeya Purana).

3. The Tantras are a diverse body of Hindu texts that explore various rituals, meditative practices, and philosophical concepts. Tantric texts often delve deeply into the worship of Shiva and Shakti, particularly in their forms as Ardhanarishvara (the androgynous deity symbolizing the union of masculine and feminine energies) and in the worship

of the divine feminine aspect known as Devi or Shakti.

4. The Upanishads are philosophical texts that explore the nature of reality, the self (Atman), and the ultimate reality (Brahman). While Shiva and Shakti are not directly discussed in the Upanishads as distinct deities, the concepts of cosmic unity and the interplay of masculine and feminine energies are foundational to Upanishadic thought.

These texts, among others, form the basis for the understanding and worship of Shiva and Shakti within Hinduism. Different sects and traditions within Hinduism may emphasize different texts and interpretations of these concepts.

The Hindu texts that mention Shiva, Shakti, and their related concepts were composed over a vast period of time, spanning thousands of years:

1. The Vedas are the oldest Hindu scriptures, composed between approximately 1500 BCE to 500 BCE. There are four Vedas: Rigveda, Samaveda, Yajurveda, and Atharvaveda. The hymns and rituals found in these texts form the basis of early Hindu religious thought.

2. The Puranas were composed over a long period, starting from around 300 BCE to as late as the 17th century CE. They are classified into different categories, and while some Puranas are earlier, others are more recent. The Shiva Purana, for example, is believed to have been composed between the 4th and 14th centuries CE.

3. The Tantras are a diverse collection of texts that emerged around the 6th century CE and continued to be composed over subsequent centuries. Tantric

practices became more prominent from around the 8th century CE onwards.

4. The Upanishads are believed to have been composed between around 800 BCE to 200 BCE, with some dating even earlier. They represent the culmination of philosophical thought within the Vedic tradition.

Ther is considerable debate among scholars regarding the exact dating of many Hindu texts. Additionally, these texts have often been transmitted orally for centuries before being written down, making precise dating challenging. As an oral tradition, the Upanishads and the Vedas predate the Old Testament by many centuries.

Conclusion

There are of course very many more papers in scientific journals that record a history of Earth going back very much earlier showing how life has evolved from simple beginnings in contrast to the special creations that YECs and ID creationists insist was the way it happened.

From Dembski's constant revisions of his disinformation and definition of terms, it looks like the Discovery Institute is giving up on trying to fool people into believing the Bible is a literal account of a six-day creation just 6-10,000 years ago, and is conceding that life changes over time, although it's not clear whether Dembski believes there was a single act of intelligent design, followed by a natural process of evolution or whether every step change in an evolving genome requires another special creation and 'infusion of information' to make sure every gene conformed to his notion of 'functional complexity' to achieve a pre-ordained objective.

I have shown how there is no evidence for the claim that biologists are on the verge of abandoning the Theory of Evolution and adopting Intelligent design creationism in its stead. That is, and has been since the early 19th century, a pipe dream of Bible literalists Christian fundamentalists. Implied claims to have discerned movements in that direction in the scientific consensus are merely the traditional false witnessing of frauds intent on misleading the public for their own political objectives – objectives which are spelled out in the Discovery Institutes Wedge Document.

The evidence for science that I have presents invariably refutes that claim in addition to refuting other aspects of creationist dogma such as the 'impossibility' of new genetic information arising, the 'absence' of 'transitional' fossils in

The Failure of Creationism

the geological column and the 'impossibility' of creating life from inorganic sources.

The evidence from history that I have presented refutes the childish notion that the Universe is a mere 6-10,000 years old and was subjected to a global genocidal flood about 4,000 years ago.

The history of humanity is several million years long involving multiple intermediate archaic forms, side-branches and interbreeding as humans spread from their birthplace in Africa across Eurasia and into the America eventually to populate every continent except Antarctica.

It is a fascinating and rewarding history to study, but most importantly, it is the story of our genes, which have spent far longer being something else that they have spent being human. For an outline of the science that traces your history from the Big Bang, read my book, *What Makes You So Special? From the Big Bang to You.*

Our genes have their origins in simple, self-replicating molecules that are passed through the sieve of selection at ever generation which only the survivors get through. They were in the single-celled archaea or the bacteria that joined forced to produce the first eukaryote cells.

They were in the first multicellular organisms and in creatures that once swam in Cambrian seas. They were in the first to creatures evolve backbones and a brain, and in the first to walk on land. They saw dinosaurs and pterodactyls and survived the mass extinction that killed the dinosaurs.

Our genes are good at surviving; they are the descendant of genes that always passed the fitness test and never once failed to produce descendants. And they are in the remarkable animal that can look up at the night sky and appreciate the enormity and wonder of it all.

Conclusion

And it is all due to the simple process of evolution, with no place for deities in the explanation. Deities should have been excised with Occam's Razor long ago.

Creationism is a failed idea, a half-baked notion that should follow phlogiston, astrology, alchemy, geocentrism and miasmas into the trash can of scientific history.

Creationism is not science; it is superstition. It has no useful function and serves no purpose other than to give frauds an excuse to fleece gullible people by selling them a false notion of their importance to a Universe that isn't even aware of their home planet, let alone of their existence. We live on a mere speck of dust in the cosmos and in Carl Saga's beautiful words:

> "That's home. That's us. On it, everyone you love, everyone you know, everyone you ever heard of, every human being who ever lived, lived out their lives. The aggregate of all our joys and sufferings, thousands of confident religions, ideologies and economic doctrines, every hunter and forager, every hero and coward, every creator and destroyer of civilizations, every king and peasant, every young couple in love, every mother and father, every hopeful child, every inventor and explorer, every teacher of morals, every corrupt politician, every superstar, every supreme leader, every saint and sinner in the history of our species, lived there on a mote of dust, suspended in a sunbeam.

> "The earth is a very small stage in a vast cosmic arena. Think of the rivers of blood spilled by all those generals and emperors so that in glory and in triumph they could become the momentary masters of a fraction of a dot. Think of the endless cruelties visited by the inhabitants of one corner of this pixel on scarcely distinguishable inhabitants of some other

The Failure of Creationism

corner of the dot. How frequent their misunderstandings, how eager they are to kill one another, how fervent their hatreds. Our posturings, our imagined self-importance, the delusion that we have some privileged position in the universe, are challenged by this point of pale light.

"Our planet is a lonely speck in the great enveloping cosmic dark. In our obscurity — in all this vastness — there is no hint that help will come from elsewhere to save us from ourselves…… It is up to us. It's been said that astronomy is a humbling, a character-building experience. To my mind, there is perhaps no better demonstration of the folly of human conceits than this distant image of our tiny world. To me, it underscores our responsibility to deal more kindly with one another and to preserve and cherish that pale blue dot, the only home we've ever known."

Carl Saga, "Pale Blue Dot"

Creationism tells you none of that.

.

Appendix I

The Predicted Demise of Evolutionary Biology

The eventual aim of the Discovery Institute's Wedge Strategy was (and still is, despite being 20 years behind schedule) replacing the Theory of Evolution (TOE) with Intelligent Design as the scientific consensus., or at least in the public perception of the scientific consensus. This was to be the prelude to abolishing the Establishment Clause in the First Amendment of the US Constitution and allowing creationism to be taught in public school science class as a legitimate science, at US taxpayers' expense.

To that end, creationists propagandists such as William Dembski, Stephen Myer[39], David Berlinski[40], James Tour[41], et

---

[39] Stephen Charles Meyer (born 1958) is an American historian, author, and former educator. He is an advocate of intelligent design, a pseudoscientific creationist argument for the existence of God. Meyer was a founder of the Center for Science and Culture (CSC) of the Discovery Institute (DI), which is the main organization behind the intelligent design movement. (Wikipedia)

[40] David Berlinski (born 1942) is an American mathematician and philosopher. He has written books about mathematics and the history of science as well as fiction. An opponent of evolution, he is a senior fellow of the Discovery Institute's Center for Science and Culture, an organization which promotes the pseudoscientific idea of intelligent design. (Wikipedia)

[41] James Mitchell Tour is an American chemist and nanotechnologist. He is a Professor of Chemistry, Professor of Materials Science and Nanoengineering at Rice University in Houston, Texas. Tour became a born-again Christian in his first year at Syracuse and identifies as a Messianic Jew. Tour signed the Scientific Dissent from Darwinism, a statement issued by the Discovery Institute disputing the scientific consensus on evolution, but, in spite of the Discovery Institute's promotion of the

al., of the major creationist organisations, have been telling the public that the TOE is a 'theory in crisis' with the scientific consensus breaking down and about to be overthrown by intelligent design as the prevailing view.

The claim that the Theory of Evolution is a theory in crisis is frequently made but their claim has many forms including the prediction that just about all of science, is about to be revealed as false and replaced by Bible literalist Christian fundamentalism. Similar predictions are regularly made by Islamic scholars in respect of Qur'anic 'science'.

In fact, modern creationists have simply taken up where previous generations of religious fundamentalists left off in this disinformation campaign, going back considerably before Darwin and Wallace's ground-breaking paper explaining their theory for how species evolved and diversified. It started almost as soon as evidence began to emerge and be widely accepted in scientific circles that the Bible was not literally true and Earth was the result of historical processes going back many tens of thousands, even millions of years.

The following list is based on that compiled initially by Glenn Moreton (53) and brought up to date (2021) by 'AnswersInScience' (54)[42]

1800's Before Darwin's TOE

1825.

"...Physical philosophy, for a long time past, had taken upon itself to deny the truth of the Mosaical statements[43], and often

---

pseudoscience of intelligent design, Tour does not consider himself to be an intelligent design proponent. (Wikipedia)
[42] Thanks to Benjamin Pierce (https://www.facebook.com/benjamin.pierce.566) for those last two sources.

Appendix I – The Predicted Demise of Evolutionary Biology

with much sarcasm, because it assigned a date of not more than about four thousand years ago, for the period of a Revolution which was able to cause marine substances to be imbedded in all parts of this inhabited earth; even in places the most remote from the sea, and in elevations very considerably above its present level. But, the progress of physical research during the last few years, conducted by naturalists of acute and honest minds, has at last terminated in so signal a concession to the testimony of the Mosaical record in this particular; that, added to the authority of Bacon's and Newton's philosophy, it renders that testimony paramount, as the rule by which all inquiries concerning revolutions general to the globe ought henceforth to be conducted. For, the mineral geology has been brought at length, by physical phenomena alone, to these conclusions; 'That the soils of all the plains were deposited in the bosom of a tranquil water; that their actual order is only to be dated from the period of the retreat of that water; that the date of that period is not very ancient; and, that it cannot be carried back above five or six thousand years.'"

Granville Penn[44], (55)

1840.

"Till within a few years, these two [Neptunism[45] and Huttonism[46]] have been the prevailing system; but another has

---

[43] The first five books of the Bible (The Pentateuch) are traditionally credited to Moses to whom God supposedly dictated them.

[44] Granville Penn (born 9 December 1761 in Spring Gardens, London) the second surviving son of Thomas Penn and his wife, Lady Juliana Fermor Penn, fourth daughter of Thomas, first Earl of Pomfret. He studied at Magdalen College, Oxford, but did not complete his degree. He then became an assistant clerk in the war department. (Wikipedia)

[45] Named after Neptune, the Roman god of the sea Neptunism, proposed by Abraham Gottlob Werner (1749–1817) was the theory that the rocks of the Earth's surface were formed by crystallization out of minerals in a vast ocean. (Wikipedia)

lately appeared which seems likely, I think, to supercede them: it is called by Mr. Granville Penn, who is its great champion, the MOSAIC GEOLOGY, because it is chiefly derived from the Mosaic History of the Creation and the Deluge."

Granville Penn (56)

"As time rolls on, new accessions of proof are unfolded; these will accumulate age by age continually, as Providence lifts the veil, until in the fulness of time, they shall merge into one mighty and irresistible blaze of truth, which will consume all the cobwebs of sophistry, and forever confound the infidel."

John Murray[47] (57)

1850

"Perhaps the author of the 'Rambles' could favour us with the induction process that converted himself; and, as the attainment of truth, and not victory, is my object, I promise either to acquiesce in or rationally refute it. Till then I hold by my antiquated tenets, that our world, nay, the whole material universe, was created about six or seven thousand years ago, and that in a state of physical excellence of which we have in our present fallen world only the 'vestiges of creation.' I conclude by mentioning that this view I have held now for nearly thirty years, and, amidst all the vicissitudes of the philosophical world during that period, I have never seen cause to change it. Of course, with this view I was, during the interval referred to, a constant opponent of the once famous, though now exploded, nebular hypothesis of La Place; and I yet expect to see physical development and long chronology

---

[46] James Hutton preceded Charles Lyell in formulating the Uniformitarian idea that Earth's geology was the result of historical forces acting over a long period of time. (Wikipedia)

[47] John Murry (c.1786-1851), archaeologist who was was interested in validating the truth of Christian scripture through archaeology. (Wikipedia)

wither also on this earth, now that THEIR ROOT (the said hypothesis) has been eradicated from the sky.[!!!]--I am, Sir, your most obedient servant,

"Philalethes." Scottish Press, cited by Hugh Miller[48], (58)

1800's Post Darwin's TOE

1871

"Long ago, when all astronomers as well as modern geologists, were against me in the then amalgamated nebular and geological hypotheses, I ventured to prophesy, and that on the principles of our starting postulates, that both these hypotheses, being spurious, were destined to succumb under the advancing light of science properly so called. One of these, and that by far the more plausible, has since become extinct. And now again I venture, (but indeed there is no venture in the case,) to repeat the same prophecy regarding the survivor, that the time is on the wing, whether we require to wait for it short or long, when it will follow its better-half to the lower regions."

Patrick M'Farlane, Esq[49]., L.M.V.I., (59)

1878

"There are some signs of this whimsical theory of Evolution soon taking another phase. Carl Vogt has given hints that perhaps they have, after all, made a mistake as to the line of descent. It may be found, he conjectures, that Man is not descended from the Ape family but from the Dog! "Other

---

[48] Hugh Miller (1802-1856) was a Scottish geologist, stone mason and fossil collector. (Wikipedia)

[49] Scottish geologist, active 1869. Author of "The Primary and Present State of the Solar System, , Particularly of Our Own Planet". (Wikipedia).

theories may soon be heard of--for the human mind is restless under the burthen of mystery."

Thomas Cooper,[50] (60)

1894

"It is true that a tide of criticism hostile to the integrity of Genesis has been rising for some years; but it seems to beat vainly against a solid rock, and the ebb has now evidently set in. The battle of historical and linguistic criticism may indeed rage for a time over the history and date of the Mosaic law, but in so far as Genesis is concerned it has been practically decided by scientific exploration."

J. William Dawson[51]. (61)

1895

"In conclusion, we venture to say that we expect one good result from the publication of Professor Prestwich's treatise, and that is that the flippant style of speaking of the Deluge, said to have been adopted in recent times by some who might, one would suppose, have known better, will henceforth be dropped; ..."

F. R. Wegg-Prosser. (62)

1900s.

1903

It must be stated that the supremacy of this philosophy has not been such as was predicted by its defenders at the outset. A

---

[50] Thomas Cooper (20 March 1805 – 15 July 1892) was an English poet and a leading Chartist who became a Baptist preacher against Darwin and for creationism. (Wikipedia)

[51] Sir John William Dawson (1820–1899) was a Canadian geologist and university administrator. (Wikipedia)

Appendix I – The Predicted Demise of Evolutionary Biology

mere glance at the history of the theory during the four decades that it has been before the public shows that the beginning of the end is at hand."

"Such utterances are now very common in the periodicals of Germany, it is said. It seems plain the reaction has commenced and that the pendulum that has swung so strongly in the direction of Evolution, is now oscillating the other way. It required twenty years for Evolution to reach us from abroad. Is it necesary [sic] for us to wait twenty years more to reverse our opinions?"

Prof. Otto Zöckler [52]. (63)

The Other Side of Evolution, 1903, p. 31-32

Cited by

Ronald L. Numbers[53]. (64)

1904

"Today, at the dawn of the new century, nothing is more certain than that Darwinism has lost its prestige among men of science. It has seen its day and will soon be reckoned a thing of the past. A few decades hence when people will look back upon the history of the doctrine of Descent, they will confess that the years between 1860 and 1880 were in many respects a time of carnival; and the enthusiasm which at that time took possession of the devotees of natural science will appear to them as the excitement attending some mad revel."

Eberhard Dennert[54]. (65)

---

[52] Professor Otto Zöckler (27 May 1833 - 19 February 1906) was a German theologian. (Wikipedia).
[53] Ronald Leslie Numbers (June 3, 1942 – July 24, 2023). American historian and opponent of creationism, a subject on which he became a leading authority. (Wikipedia).

Cited by Ronald L. Numbers (op. cit)

1905

Collapse of Evolution (66).

Luther Tracy Townsend[55]

1910s

1912

" It was this independent research in a very wide field of thought that led me to enlarge the pamphlet of 1874 to a book of 400 pages in 1885; and again it was revised and enlarged in 1902; and I have been greatly encouraged by the fact that this last edition is now used in some of the colleges, and in at least two universities as an educator. "

"When the first volume was published in 1874 it was a rare thing to meet with a scientist who would admit that the earth had a ring system; to-day it is as rare to meet with one who does not concede the great fact, and the great problem is resolving itself into this form: How did the earth's rings fall back to the surface of the planet?"

Isaac Newton Vail[56] (67),

"The word evolution is in itself innocent enough, and has a large range of legitimate use. The Bible, indeed, teaches a system of evolution. The world was not made in an instant, or even in one day (whatever period day may signify) but in six

---

[54] Eberhard Dennert (1861-1942) was a German natural scientist and philosopher. (Wikipedia)

[55] Reverend Luther Tracy Townsend (September 27, 1838 - 1922) was a professor at Boston University and an author of theological and historical works. (Wikipedia)

[56] Isaac Newton Vail (1840 – January 26, 1912) was an American Quaker, schoolteacher, and pseudoscientist supporting the theory of catastrophism. His ideas were taken up by creationists including Jehovah's Witnesses. (Wikipedia)

days. Throughout the whole process there was an orderly progress from lower to higher forms of matter and life. In short there is an established *order* in all the Creator's work. Even the Kingdom of Heaven is like a grain of mustard seed which being planted grew from the smallest beginnings to be a tree in which the fowls of heaven could take refuge [Luke 13:19]. So everywhere there is "first the blade, then the ear, then the full corn in the ear" [Mark 4:28].

But recently the word has come into much deserved disrepute by the injection into it of erroneous and harmful theological and philosophical implications. The widely current doctrine of evolution which we are now compelled to combat is one which practically eliminates God from the whole creative process and relegates mankind to the tender mercies of a mechanical universe the wheels of whose machinery are left to move on without any immediate Divine direction…

…In short, everything points to the unity of the human race, and to the fact that, while built on the general pattern of the higher animals associated with him in the later geological ages, he differs from them in so many all important particulars, that it is necessary to suppose that he came into existence as the Bible represents, by the special creation of a single pair, from whom all the varieties of the race have sprung.

George Frederick Wright[57]. (68)

1920s

1922

"The science of twenty or thirty years ago was in high glee at the thought of having almost proved the theory of biological

---

[57] George Frederick Wright (January 22, 1838 – April 20, 1921) was an American geologist and a professor at Oberlin Theological Seminary. (Wikipedia).

evolution. Today, for every careful, candid inquirer, these hopes are crushed; and with weary, reluctant sadness does modern biology now confess that the Church has probably been right all the time"

George McCready Price[58],

quoted in J. E. Conant's The Church The Schools And Evolution (1922), p.18 (69)

This this was a barefaced lie can be seen in the response of the American Association for the Advancement of Science to McCready's claim;

> *Since it has been asserted that there is not a fact in the universe in support of this theory, that it is a "mere guess" which leading scientists are now abandoning, and that even the American Association for the Advancement of Science at its last meeting in Toronto, Canada, approved this revolt against evolution, and*
>
> *Inasmuch as such statements have been given wide publicity through the press and are misleading public opinion on this subject, therefore,*
>
> *The Council of the American Association for the Advancement of Science has thought it advisable to take formal steps upon this matter, in order that there may be no ground for misunderstanding of the attitude of this Association, which is one of the largest scientific bodies in the world, with a membership of more than 11,000 persons, including the American*

---

[58] George McCready Price (26 August 1870 – 24 January 1963) A Canadian creationist who produced several anti-evolution and creationist works, particularly on the subject of flood geology. His views did not become common among creationists until after his death, particularly with the modern 'creation science' movement starting in the 1960s.(Wikipedia).

Appendix I – The Predicted Demise of Evolutionary Biology

> *authorities in all branches of science. The following statements represent the position of the Council with regard to the theory of evolution.*
>
> *The Council of the Association affirms that, so far as the scientific evidences of evolution of plants and animals and man are concerned, there is no ground whatever for the assertion that these evidences constitute a "mere guess." No scientific generalization is more strongly supported by thoroughly tested evidences than is that of organic evolution."* (70)

1924

"…I am convinced that science is making substantial progress. Darwinism has been definitely outgrown. As a doctrine it is merely of historical interest. True, the current teaching of geology still occupy the center of the stage, and the real modern discoveries which completely discredit these teachings are only beginning to get a hearing. The New Catastrophism is the theory of tomorrow in the science of geology; and under the teaching of this new view of geology the whole theory of evolution will take its place with the many 'perishing dreams and the wrecks of forgotten deliriums'. And at that time the entire teaching of science along these lines will be found to be in complete harmony with the opening chapters of the Ancient Hebrew Scriptures. 'In the beginning God created the heaven and the earth."

George McCready Price,

quoted in Alexander Hardie's Evolution: Is It Philosophical, Scientific Or Scriptural? (1924), pp.125-126 (71)

1929

"The world has had enough of evolution … In the future, evolution will be remembered only as the crowning deception which the arch-enemy of human souls foisted upon the race in his attempt to lead man away from the Savior. The Science of the future will be creationism. As the ages roll by, the mysteries of creation week will be cleared up, and as we have learned to read the secrets of creative power in the lives of animals and plants about us, we shall understand much that our dim senses cannot now fathom. If we hope to continue scientific study in the laboratories and fields of the earth restored, we must begin to get the lessons of truth now. The time is ripe for a rebellion against the dominion of evolution, and for a return to the fundamentals of true science,"

Harold W. Clark[59] (72).

1930s

1935

The chain of evidence that purports to support the theory of evolution is a chain indeed, but its links are formed of sand and mist. Analyze the evidence and it melts away; turn the light of true investigation upon its demonstrations and they fade like fog before the freshening breeze. The theory stands today positively disproved, and we will venture the prophecy that in another two decades, when younger men, free from the blind prejudices of a passing generation are allowed to investigate the new evidence, examine the facts, and form their own conclusions, the theory will take its place in the limbo of disproved tidings. In that day the world of science will be forced to come back to the unshakable foundation of fact that is the basis of the true philosophy of the origin of life."

Harry Rimmer (73)[60]

---

[59] Harold Willard Clark (Born::1891-Died::1986) was a Berkeley-trained biologist and a former student of George McCready Price who later replaced him on the faculty of Pacific Union College in 1922. Clark ultimately taught biology at Seventh-Day Adventist colleges for thirty-five years. (Wikipedia).

Appendix I – The Predicted Demise of Evolutionary Biology

1940

The Bible is the one foundation on which all true science must finally rest: because it is the one book of ultimate origins. Science established on this foundation will endure. In fact, there can be no true science without this foundation. False science must fall. Already, its decline is evident."

L. Allen Higley. (74)[61]

1960s

1961

"I suspect that the creationist has less mystery to explain away than the wholehearted evolutionist. On the balance of the things that I have both read and discovered for myself I am a creationist, so far as mega-evolution is concerned. By mega-evolution one refers to the origin of kingdoms, phyla, classes and orders, the largest groups in any classification of living things. I concede micro-evolution, of course, which is the origin by evolutionary processes of species, genera, and even families. An increasing number of thoughtful scientists seem to be adopting this view, which I should add is decades old, and far from being original."

Evan Shute.[62] (75)

---

[60] Harry Rimmer (1890–1952) was an American evangelist and creationist. He is most prominent as a defender of creationism in the United States, a fundamentalist leader and writer of anti-evolution publications. (Wikipedia)

[61] Louis Allen Higley (1871-1955) taught science at Wheaton from 1924 to 1939 and was an outspoken advocate of gap (ruin - restoration) harmonization of the biblical creation account and modern science. (ResearchGate)

[62] Evan Vere Shute (October 21, 1905 – 1978) F.R.C.S.C. was a Canadian obstetrician, poet and writer best known for advocating vitamin E therapy to treat cardiovascular disease and many other diseases. His studies were not controlled and his results were not

1963

"In spite of the tremendous pressure that exists in the scientific world on the side of evolutionary propaganda, there are increasing signs of discontent and skepticism"

"Here and there, surprisingly enough, even in the standard scientific publications media, there are beginning to appear evidences of doubts concerning evolution. Nothing much which is overtly skeptical of evolution as a whole can be published, of course, but at least signs are appearing which indicate there may exist a very substantial substratum of doubt concerning evolution today.

Henry Morris.[63] (76)

1970s

1970

"Indeed, of late, more and more have come to recognize not only the reality but also the importance of the spiritual. Dryden says that scientists have come to realize that atrophy of the moral and spiritual life is inconsistent with well-rounded development."

John W. Klotz.[64] (77)

---

confirmed by other medical researchers.(Wikipedia)

[63] Henry Madison Morris (October 6, 1918 – February 25, 2006) was an American young Earth creationist, Christian apologist and engineer. He was one of the founders of the Creation Research Society and the Institute for Creation Research. He is considered by many to be "the father of modern creation science" (Wikipedia)

[64] Dr. John Klotz, PhD. in Biology, was a noted Lutheran pastor, theologian and student of the sciences. Dr. Klotz was one of the first Lutheran pastors in the Missouri Synod to obtain an advanced degree in the sciences precisely for the sake of being able to engage in intelligent conversation and analysis of the modern sciences, informed by a profound commitment to God's Word and the

Appendix I – The Predicted Demise of Evolutionary Biology

1975

"QUESTION--Do non-Christian scientists still argue that man has descended from apes or monkeys?

ANSWER--In many school textbooks this is accepted almost as if it is fact, but many biologists and other scientists have long since swung away from this view. There are many and varied theories of evolution today, but scientists who reject divine creation are beset with serious problems and these are being increasingly recognized."

Clifford Wilson[65] (78)

1976

"But even at that time there were some evolutionists who were beginning to express doubts concerning this formulation of evolution theory. A decade later, these incipient cracks have widened to the point that some, formerly strongly committed to this theory, are now expressing disillusionment."

Duane T. Gish.[66] (79)

1980s

1984

Lutheran Confessions. (Amazon.com – Author information)
[65] Dr. Clifford A. Wilson (1923-2012) was an Australian young-earth creationist archaeologist, author, and psycholinguist. He was formerly the Director of the Australian Institute of Archaeology (1967-70), and then served as senior lecturer at Monash University in Melbourne, Australia. (CreationWiki)
[66] Duane Tolbert Gish (February 17, 1921 – March 5, 2013) was an American biochemist and a prominent member of the creationist movement. A young Earth creationist, Gish was a former vice-president of the Institute for Creation Research (ICR) and the author of numerous publications about creation science. (Wikipedia)

The Failure of Creationism

"Furthermore, even if it wasn't clear in Darwin's day, the modern scientific creationist movement has made it abundantly clear in our day that all the real facts of science support this Biblical position. Despite all the bombastic books and articles, both by secular evolutionists and compromising evangelicals, which have opposed the modern literature on scientific Biblical creationism/catastrophism, the evidence is sound, and more and more scientists are becoming creationists all the time."

Henry M. Morris (80),

"One of the encouraging signs of our day is to see the large number of young people who are beginning to realize they are being manipulated by the educational system. In my lectures on university campuses and elsewhere, I am encouraged by the increasing awareness of young people to this problem. More and more young scientists are interested in searching out the creationist explanation for origins and earth history. Some excellent creationist research is also being accomplished by these young people even at the graduate level. They are not receiving much encouragement from the educational establishment, but they are going ahead anyway."

Donald E. Chittick.[67] (81)

1987

"Evolution is in absolute chaos today and has been especially for this decade of the '80's. The '80's has been extremely bad for Evolution. Every major pillar of Evolution has crumbled in the decade of the '80's."

---

[67] Dr. Donald E. Chittick has been active in creation apologetics missions for more than forty years. He has written several books including his recently revised book, *The Puzzle of Ancient Man*, his highly acclaimed, *The Controversy: Roots of the Creation-Evolution Conflict*, and *The World and Time: Age and History of the Earth*. He, along with his wife Donna, run a creation ministry called Creation Compass.

Appendix I – The Predicted Demise of Evolutionary Biology

D. James Kennedy.[68] (82)

1988

"Hundreds of scientists who once taught their university students that the bottom line on origins had finally been figured out and settled are today confessing that they were completely wrong. They have discovered that their previous conclusions, once held so fervently, were based on very fragile evidences and suppositions which have since been refuted by new discoveries. This has necessitated a change in their basic philosophical position on origins. Others are admitting great weaknesses in evolution theory. One of the world's most highly respected philosophers of science, Dr. Karl Popper, has argued that one theory of origins, almost universally accepted as a scientific fact, does not even qualify as a scientific theory. A 1980 display at the prestigious British Museum of Natural History made the same admission."

"Leading scientists are abandoning their faith in Darwin's theory of evolution. Why?" (back cover notes)

Luther D. Sunderland.[69] (83)

---

[68] Dennis James Kennedy (November 3, 1930 – September 5, 2007) was an American Presbyterian pastor, evangelist, Christian broadcaster, and author. He was the senior pastor of Coral Ridge Presbyterian Church in Fort Lauderdale, Florida, from 1960 until his death in 2007. Kennedy also founded Evangelism Explosion International, and the Center for Reclaiming America for Christ, a socially conservative political group. (Wikipedia)

[69] LUTHER D. SUNDERLAND, B.S. (Penn State University), an aerospace engineer with the General Electric Company, was involved for 30 years with the research and development of automatic flight control systems (autopilots) for a number of aircraft such as the F-111, Boeing 757 and 767. He was elected to the engineering honor society Tau Beta Pi, is an Associate Fellow in the American Institute for Aeronautics and Astronautics, authored many published articles and papers on aviation, and holds a number of patents in his field. (Creationism.org)

The Failure of Creationism

Note: Karl Popper recanted his view of the Theory of Evolution in 1978 (84), ten years before Sunderland misrepresented his views, with:

> *The fact that the theory of natural selection is difficult to test has led some people, anti-Darwinists and even some great Darwinists, to claim that it is a tautology. . . . . I mention this problem because I too belong among the culprits. Influenced by what these authorities say, I have in the past described the theory as "almost tautological," and I have tried to explain how the theory of natural selection could be untestable (as is a tautology) and yet of great scientific interest. My solution was that the doctrine of natural selection is a most successful metaphysical research programme. . . . [Popper, 1978, p. 344]*
>
> *I have changed my mind about the testability and logical status of the theory of natural selection; and I am glad to have an opportunity to make a recantation. . . . [p. 345]*
>
> *The theory of natural selection may be so formulated that it is far from tautological. In this case it is not only testable, but it turns out to be not strictly universally true. There seem to be exceptions, as with so many biological theories; and considering the random character of the variations on which natural selection operates, the occurrence of exceptions is not surprising. [p. 346]*

This lie was first recorded by Duane T. Gish in 1981, three years after Popper's recantation. It continues to be cited today.

1989

Although the history of the earth and life has long been interpreted by the uniformitarian maxim, 'the present is the key to the past,' more and more geologists are returning to catastrophism."

Henry M. Morris (85)

1990s (Pre-Wedge[70])

"Even though the large majority of modern scientists still embrace an evolutionary view of origins, there is a significant and growing number of scientists who have abandoned evolution altogether and have accepted creation instead."

Mark Looy.[71] (86)

1991

Of course, the demise of the Big Bang theory will not discourage evolutionary theorists from proposing other theories. In fact, theories based on plasma processes and a revised steady-state theory have already been advanced to replace Big Bang cosmologies."

Duane T. Gish (87),

1993

"Today, there is a growing recognition among scientists of the dramatic implication that the principle of uniformity holds for the origin of functional information. This is not an argument against Darwinian evolution. It is, however, an important scientific inference in favor of the intelligent origin of genetic messages...

---

[70] The Wedge Strategy is the Discovery Institute's plan to use evolution as the thin end of a wedge to turn American public opinion against 'materialist' science and for fundamentalist Christianity to facilitate removal of the Establishment Clause from the US Constitution, with the long-term aim of a fundamentalist theocracy in the USA.
[71] Co-founder of Answers in Genesis, with Ken Ham

"Today, however, the 'creative' role of natural selection is being questioned by a growing number of scientists. Yet most of these scientists have not reconsidered the intelligent design argument which was replaced by natural selection as the supposed source of apparent design."

Percival Davis[72] and Dean H. Kenyon.[73] (88)

"There are hopeful signs, however. Evolution theory itself has now collapsed under scientific scrutiny. Further, the foundations have not been totally abandoned by scientists."

T. V. Varughese.[74] (89)

1994

"Even scientists are leaving Darwinian evolution in droves, recognizing that strictly natural processes, operating at random on inorganic chemicals, could never have produced complex living cells. They have grown weary of arguing how random mutations in a highly complex genetic code provide improvements in it."

John D. Morris.[75] (90)

---

[72] Percival William Davis, also known as Bill Davis, is an American author, young earth creationist, and intelligent design proponent. (Wikipedia).

[73] Dean H. Kenyon (born c. 1939) is an American biophysicist who is Professor Emeritus of Biology at San Francisco State University, a young Earth creationist, and one of the founders of the intelligent design movement. He is the author of *Biochemical Predestination*.

[74] T.V. Varughese, Ph.D., is a creationist author and academic associated with Christian and apologetic perspectives. He holds a doctorate and has worked as an Associate Professor of Computer Science at National University in Irvine, California, and as an adjunct professor of Physics at the Institute for Creation Research (ICR).(ChatGPT in response to user question)

[75] John David Morris (7 December 1946 – 29 January 2023) was an American young earth creationist. He was the son of "the father of creation science", Henry M. Morris, and served as president of the Institute for Creation Research (ICR) from the time of his

Appendix I – The Predicted Demise of Evolutionary Biology

"Well, the Big Bang has started to fizzle! Astronomer Hoyle says that a 'sickly pall now hangs over the big bang theory.' The Big Bang has fallen with a big bang! Eminent scientists who reject the BBT include Nobel Prize winner Hannes Alfven[76], astronomer Sir Fred Hoyle[77], astronomer Jayant Narlikar[78], astronomer N. Chandra Wickramasinghe[79], astronomer Geoffrey Burbidge, physicist Allen Allen, physicist Hermann Bondi, physicist Robert Oldershaw and physicist G. de Vaucouleurs."

Don Boys.[80] (91)

---

father's retirement in 1996 until 2020.

[76] Hannes Olof Gösta Alfvén (30 May 1908 – 2 April 1995) was a Swedish electrical engineer, plasma physicist and winner of the 1970 Nobel Prize in Physics for his work on magnetohydrodynamics (MHD) (Wikipedia)

[77] Sir Fred Hoyle FRS (24 June 1915 – 20 August 2001) was an English astronomer who formulated the theory of stellar nucleosynthesis and was one of the authors of the influential B²FH paper. He also held controversial stances on other scientific matters—in particular his rejection of the "Big Bang" theory (a term coined by him on BBC Radio) in favor of the "steady-state model", and his promotion of panspermia as the origin of life on Earth. (Wikipedia).

[78] Jayant Vishnu Narlikar FNA, FASc, FTWAS (born 19 July 1938) is an Indian astrophysicist and emeritus professor at the Inter-University Centre for Astronomy and Astrophysics (IUCAA). He developed with Sir Fred Hoyle the conformal gravity theory, known as Hoyle–Narlikar theory. (Wikipedia)

[79] Nalin Chandra Wickramasinghe MBE (born 20 January 1939) is a Sri Lankan-born British mathematician, astronomer and astrobiologist of Sinhalese ethnicity. His research interests include the interstellar medium, infrared astronomy, light scattering theory, applications of solid-state physics to astronomy, the early Solar System, comets, astrochemistry, the origin of life and astrobiology. (Wikipedia)

[80] Don Boys, Ph.D. was born in West Virginia, and received his early education there. He was educated at Moody Bible Institute,

The Failure of Creationism

Notice how none of Don Boy's 'experts' are biologists!

1995

"The cosmologists (with a number of notable exceptions) are all committed to the 'Big Bang' theory of cosmic origin, the date of which is the age for which they are searching. But the 'Big Bang' itself is highly speculative, and there are a growing number of astronomers who are questioning it."

Henry M. Morris (92)

"Of course, I take a different view. In my opinion, much of the history of the twentieth century will be seen in retrospect as a failed experiment in scientific atheism. The thinkers most responsible for making the twentieth century mindset were Darwin, Marx, and Freud. Freud has now lost most of his scientific standing, and Marx has been so spectacularly discredited that he retains his influence only in the loftiest academic ivory towers. Darwinism is still untouchable, but the most widely used college evolutionary biology textbook (by Douglas Futuyma[81]) links his achievement to that of the other two. "

Phillip E. Johnson[82] (93)

Tennessee Temple College, Immanuel College and Seminary and Heritage Baptist University where he earned his Ph.D. (Amazon.com Author biography)

[81] Douglas Joel Futuyma (born 24 April 1942) is an American evolutionary biologist. He is a Distinguished Professor in the Department of Ecology and Evolution at Stony Brook University in Stony Brook, New York and a Research Associate on staff at the American Museum of Natural History in New York City.

[82] Phillip E. Johnson (June 18, 1940 – November 2, 2019) was an American legal scholar who was the Jefferson E. Peyser Professor of Law at the University of California, Berkeley. He was an opponent of evolutionary science, co-founder of the Discovery Institute's Center for Science and Culture (CSC), and one of the co-founders of the intelligent design movement, along with William Dembski and

Appendix I – The Predicted Demise of Evolutionary Biology

1996

"We are the only people ever to see (or need) direct scientific proof not only of God's existence, but also for His transcendent capacity to create space and time dimensions, as well as to operate in dimensions independent from our own four."

Hugh Ross.[83] (94)

"The Behe argument is as revolutionary for our time as was Darwin's argument was for his. If true, it presages not just a change in a scientific theory, but an overthrow of the worldview that has dominated intellectual life ever since the triumph of Darwinism, the metaphysical doctrine of scientific materialism or naturalism. A lot is at stake, and not just for science."

Phillip E. Johnson (95)

1997

"In the not-so-distant future, when someone of the stature of a Stephen Jay Gould[84] or the late Carl Sagan[85] holds a press conference to announce he has finally reached the conclusion

---

Michael Behe. Johnson described himself as "in a sense the father of the intelligent design movement. (Wikipedia)

[83] Hugh Norman Ross (born July 24, 1945) is a Canadian astrophysicist, Christian apologist, and old-Earth creationist.(Wikipedia)

[84] Stephen Jay Gould (September 10, 1941 – May 20, 2002) was an American palaeontologist, evolutionary biologist, and historian of science. He was one of the most influential and widely read authors of popular science of his generation.

[85] Carl Edward Sagan (November 9, 1934 – December 20, 1996) was an American astronomer, planetary scientist and science communicator. His best known scientific contribution is his research on the possibility of extraterrestrial life, including experimental demonstration of the production of amino acids from basic chemicals by exposure to light.

that evolution is scientifically bankrupt, other scientists will quickly follow suit. It'll resemble rats deserting a sinking ship. And with the publication of Behe's book, Berlinski's articles, and December's stunning announcement that *Homo erectus* and *Homo sapiens* may have lived at the same time, I think I'm beginning to hear the sounds of tiny feet scampering over the decks. Can you?"

David Buckna[86] (96)

(It's not immediately obvious why *H. sapiens* being contemporaneous with *H. erectus* for part of their history is a problem for the Theory of Evolution)

Discovery Institute's "Wedge Strategy" drafted

1990s (Post-Wedge)

1998

"Darwin gave us a creation story, one in which God was absent and undirected natural processes did all the work. That creation story has held sway for more than a hundred years. It is now on the way out. When it goes, so will all the edifices that have been built on its foundation."

William A. Dembski (97)

"What is science going to look like once intelligent design replaces it?"

William A. Dembski (98)

---

[86] David Buckna is a Canadian educator and creationist known for his critiques of evolutionary theory, particularly in the context of science education. As a public school teacher, Buckna has advocated for presenting creationism and criticisms of evolution alongside evolutionary theory in educational settings. He has written numerous articles for Answers in Genesis, where he questions mainstream scientific consensus on evolution and argues for intelligent design, contending that evolutionary explanations fail to account for the complexity and diversity of life.

Appendix I – The Predicted Demise of Evolutionary Biology

Of Evolution:

"In appearance it is as impregnable as the Soviet Union seemed a few years ago. But the ship has sprung a metaphysical leak, and that leak widens as more and more people understand it and draw attention to the conflict between empirical science and materialist philosophy. The more perceptive of the ship's officers know that the ship is doomed if the leak cannot be plugged. The struggle to save the ship will go on for a while, and meanwhile there will even be academic wine-and-cheese parties on the deck. In the end the ship's great firepower and ponderous armor will only help drag it to the bottom."

Phillip Johnson (99)

1999

"Meanwhile, it is my personal hope that these positions newly adopted by scholars in the scientific community when they do reach the larger world, will lead to turn to a renewal of philosophy and humane letters, and that an enhanced confidence in the ordered structure of physical reality will afford men and women a more assured, firmer stride in the paths of narrative and poetic composition. Actually, I have no doubt that this will be the case, at least after my time, and I cherish the suspicion that future students of literary history, not so terribly far down the road, may look back to these past two centuries as a somewhat weird period, during which an extraordinary multitude of singularly disturbed authors composed an inordinate number of very bizarre and disquieting books. 'Yes,' their teachers will be obliged to inform them, 'a lot of people back in those unfortunate days had gotten it into their silly heads that the whole world and everything in it had somehow evolved by accident, you see. It was all rather strange."

Patrick Henry Reardon[87] (100)

2000s

(A number of the cited websites appear to have been taken down, perhaps understandable, as no-one in fundamentalist theology like to be identified as a false prophet)

"There is growing interest in a biological theory of intelligent design around the world. While many still vigorously oppose all such ideas, there is a much greater openness than ever before. Philosophers, mathematicians, chemists, engineers, and biologists are willing to suggest, even demand, that a more rigorous study of intelligent design in relation to biological organisms be pursued. A renaissance may be around the corner."

Ray Bohlin[88] (101)

2001

"Nevertheless, evolutionists, having largely become disenchanted with the fossil record as a witness for evolution because of the ubiquitous gaps where there should be transitions, recently have been promoting DNA and other genetic evidence as proof of evolution."

Henry M. Morris (102)

---

[87] Patrick Henry Reardon is an archpriest of the Antiochian Orthodox Christian Archdiocese, author, lecturer, podcaster, and senior editor of *Touchstone*.

[88] Raymond Bohlin is a Research Fellow of the Discovery Institute's Center for the Renewal of Science and Culture, and thus deeply involved in pushing intelligent design creationism as a scientifically valid alternative to evolution for America's school children (not as a scientifically valid alternative to evolution for *scientists*, since that would require, you know, science and evidence and research and stuff, and these guys aren't into *that*). (Encyclopedia of American Loons #509)

Appendix I – The Predicted Demise of Evolutionary Biology

"Intellectual honesty will soon force many scientists to abandon Darwin's theory of the evolution of species in exchange for intelligent design or outright Biblical creation."

Gregory J. Brewer[89] (103)

2002

"Creation scientists may be in the minority so far, but their number is growing, and most of them (like this writer) were evolutionists at one time, having changed to creationism at least in part because of what they decided was the weight of scientific evidence."

Henry M. Morris. (104)

"As the evidence mounts, many biologists and others are returning to a belief in a Creation-God."

"The good news is that the ever-increasing acquisition of knowledge is now pointing scientists back to God! Based on historical factors, eventually that belief will filter down to the schools and the general public."

"Others may fear a need to change their lifestyles to please a God. Still others make their livelihood trying to prove naturalistic evolution. There are many possible reasons, yet the scientific trend, particularly in microbiology, is a return to consideration of God."

Ralph O. Muncaster[90] (105)

---

[89] Gregory J. Brewer, affiliated with the Institute for Creation Research (ICR), holds a B.S. in Biology from the California Institute of Technology and a Ph.D. in Biology from the University of California. Brewer has written on topics challenging Darwinian evolution and promoting intelligent design, notably in his article "The Imminent Death of Darwinism and the Rise of Intelligent Design" published by ICR.(ChatGPT4o response to user question)
[90] Ralph O. Muncaster is a former atheist and Bible skeptic who became a prominent Christian apologist and creationist. His journey

The Failure of Creationism

2003

"In fact, the common presupposition that evolution is right may soon be behind us." (106)

"However, in 1991, Mayr boldly stated, 'There is probably no biologist left today who would question that all organisms now found on the earth have descended from a single origin of life.' In the ten years since Mayr made this statement, however, support for it has been shattered."

Ralph O. Muncaster. (106)

"What should one make of these evolutionary controversies among atheists? The individuals engaging in the controversies would tell us that these are simply family fights about details. Just be patient, they explain, and all the controversies will be resolved in favor of a universe in which God is irrelevant. My view is that several of the disputes appear to be about basics, not details. And I think there is some probability that the entire paradigm may come crashing down at some time in the future."

Henry F. Schaefer.[91] (107)

---

to faith involved investigating the Bible with the intention of disproving it, but he ultimately found what he viewed as compelling evidence supporting biblical accuracy, including its prophetic elements. Muncaster went on to establish the Institute of Contemporary Christian Faith, where he aims to help others explore Christianity and understand creationist perspectives. (ChatGPT4o response to user request)

[91] Henry Frederick "Fritz" Schaefer III (born June 8, 1944) is an American computational, physical, and theoretical chemist. He is one of the most highly cited chemists in the world, with a Thomson Reuters h-index of 121 as of 2020... Schaefer is an active Protestant Christian educator who regularly speaks to university audiences (over 500 to date), Christian groups and the public on science/faith issues (Wikipedia).

Appendix I – The Predicted Demise of Evolutionary Biology

"As a result of the tremendous advances in the study of genetics, molecular biology, and the acknowledgement that the fossil record does not provide any support for the theory of evolution, a growing number of scientists have either publicly rejected evolution or have expressed very serious reservations about Darwin's theory."

"In fact, the scientific problems and inconsistencies of the theory of evolution are so overwhelmingly obvious that it now faces collapse on all fronts. The only thing holding the tattered theory of evolution together is the powerful desire of millions of people to hold on to the notion of evolution regardless of its scientific weakness, because the alternative is unthinkable to its practitioners."

Grant R. Jeffrey.[92] (108)

2004

"History seems to be repeating itself. Just as the first Darwinists gave up on the earliest versions of abiogenesis, so scientists today are abandoning long-cherished pillars of the naturalistic origin-of-life paradigm. Many now speculate that life may have originated somewhere other than on Earth."

Fazale Rana[93] and Hugh Ross. (109)

"At the time, Darwin offered a powerful vision for understanding biology and therewith the world. That vision is now faltering, and a new vision is offering to replace it."

---

[92] Grant Reid Jeffrey (October 5, 1948 – May 11, 2012) was a Canadian Bible teacher of Bible prophecy/eschatology and biblical archaeology and a proponent of dispensational evangelical Christianity. (Wikipedia)

[93] Fazale "Fuz" Rana (born February 6, 1963) is an American biochemist, Christian Apologist, author, and science lecturer. Since July 2022, he has advanced from the position of Vice President to become the President and CEO of Reasons to Believe, a nonprofit organization that promotes day-age forms of old Earth creationism.(Wikipedia)

"Yes, we are interested in and write about the theological and cultural implications of Darwinism's imminent demise and replacement by intelligent design."

William A. Dembski. (110)

"In the next five years, molecular Darwinism -- the idea that Darwinian processes can produce complex molecular structures at the subcellular level -- will be dead. When that happens, evolutionary biology will experience a crisis of confidence because evolutionary biology hinges on the evolution of the right molecules. I therefore foresee a Taliban-style collapse of Darwinism in the next ten years."

William Dembski, (111)

World Magazine published a series of articles on what the world would look like in 2025. This classic statement came from an article by Phillip Johnson.

"The collapse of the Soviet Union put an end to the Soviet myth, just as the scientific collapse of Darwinism, preceded as it was by the discrediting of Marxism and Freudianism, prepared the way for the culture to turn aside from the mythology of naturalism to rediscover the buried treasure that the mythology had been concealing."

Phillip E. Johnson. (112)

"Now, a mere quarter of a century later, Darwinian evolution is little more than a historical footnote in biology textbooks. Just as students learn that scientists used to believe that the Sun moves around the Earth and maggots are spontaneously generated in rotting meat, so students also learn that scientists used to believe that human beings evolved through random mutations and natural selection. How could a belief that was so influential in 2000 become so obsolete by 2025? Whatever happened to evolutionary theory?"

Jonathan Wells.[94] (113)

Appendix I – The Predicted Demise of Evolutionary Biology

"The house of evolution is falling. Its various theorists are increasingly at war with each other over the basic question of how evolution is supposed to work, and its materialistic and naturalistic foundation is becoming increasingly clear. The evolutionists tenaciously hold to their theory on the basis of faith and as an axiom of their worldview. The publication of these two articles in influential magazines indicates that proponents of evolution see the Intelligent Design movement as a real threat. They are right."

R. Albert Mohler, Jr.[95] (114)

2005

"I think whether it's our case or some other case Darwin's going down the tube. ... No question about it."

Richard Thompson of the Thomas More Law Center[96], (115)

2006

"I see this all disintegrating very quickly,"

William A. Dembski (116)

---

[94] John Corrigan "Jonathan" Wells (September 19, 1942 – September 19, 2024) was an American biologist, theologian, and advocate of the pseudoscientific argument of intelligent design. Wells joined the Unification Church in 1974, and subsequently wrote that the teachings of its founder Sun Myung Moon and his own studies at the Unification Theological Seminary and his prayers convinced him to devote his life to "destroying Darwinism." (Wikipedia)

[95] Dr. R. Albert Mohler Jr. serves as president of The Southern Baptist Theological Seminary – the flagship school of the Southern Baptist Convention and one of the largest seminaries in the world. Dr. Mohler has been recognized by such influential publications as *Time*, calling him the "reigning intellectual of the evangelical movement in the U.S." (https://albertmohler.com/about/)

[96] Defending the Dover Area School Board in the Kitzmiller Case.

"It's almost not worth deciding what to do about Darwinism, because it is on the way out anyway."

Denyse O'Leary.[97] (117)

"...the universe was designed for discovery. And with each discovery, the Darwinian theory of evolution is expected to go down as 'a huge mistake in history,'

Jay Richards.[98] (118)

2007

"In fact, an appreciable number of perfectly reasonable biologists are coming to think that the theory of natural selection can no longer be taken for granted. This is, so far, mostly straws in the wind; but it's not out of the question that a scientific revolution - no less than a major revision of evolutionary theory - is in the offing."

Jerry Fodor[99]. (119)

"It is not too early to chart the intellectual course to the 22nd century. The 21st century may well mark a gradual disaffection with Darwinism, comparable to the 20th century's loss of support for Marxism."

Steve Fuller[100]. (120)

---

[97] Denyse O'Leary (not to be confused with Denis Leary) is a Canadian intelligent design apologist who claims to be a journalist. (RationalWiki)

[98] Jay Wesley Richards is an American analytical philosopher who focuses on the intersection of politics, philosophy, and religion. He is the William E. Simon Senior Research Fellow in Heritage's DeVos Center for Religion and Civil Society at The Heritage Foundation. (Wikipedia)

[99] Jerry Alan Fodor (April 22, 1935 – November 29, 2017) was an American philosopher and the author of many crucial works in the fields of philosophy of mind and cognitive science.

[100] Steve William Fuller (born 1959) is an American social philosopher in the field of science and technology studies. He has

Appendix I – The Predicted Demise of Evolutionary Biology

2008

"We live in exciting times. The Darwinist/materialist hegemony over our culture has definitely peaked, and we are privileged to watch the initial tremors that are shaking the Darwinist house of cards. These are only the beginning of woes for St. Charles' disciples, and I look forward to one day watching the entire rotten edifice come crashing down. I am persuaded that just as when the Soviet Union went seemingly overnight from -menacing colossus astride the globe- to -non-existent,- the final crash of the House of Darwin will happen with astonishing suddenness. You can be sure that we at UD will be there not only reporting on events, but also lending our intellectual pry bars to the effort."

Barry Arrington[101]. (121)

2019

"If you ask your typical garden variety evolutionist, he will tell you that all is well in the land of Darwinia. But if you look behind the right curtains, you find that some highly placed, mainstream evolutionary biologists concede that neo-Darwinism is in deep crisis. They acknowledge its imminent fall even as they cling to the hope that some purely blind, materialistic version of evolution can be cobbled together to replace it."

Marcos Eberlin[102] (122)

---

published in the areas of social epistemology, academic freedom, and in support of intelligent design and transhumanism.

[101] Barry Arrington is a lawyer from Arvada, Colorado who is associated with William Dembski and the "Michele PAC." He basically seems like the lawyer for the middle management agents of conservative right wing thought (read: nuttiness) in the United States….Arrington has claimed that using the fossil record to argue for evolution is cheating since the fossil record is based on science.(RationalWiki)

[102] Marcos Nogueira Eberlin (born 4 March 1959) is a Brazilian

2024

"Origin of life researchers are starting to question seriously neo-Darwinism and leaning towards the better scientific theory of intelligent design. I remain an eternal optimist. Just this past week, an article entitled "How Science Suggests God May Have Created the Universe" flashed across my newsfeed.

Gregory J. Rummo.[103] (123)

---

chemist and former professor at the Institute of Chemistry of the University of Campinas. He is a member of the Brazilian Academy of Sciences and received the Brazilian National Order of Scientific Merit in 2005 and the Thomson Medal in 2016... Eberlin is an advocate of intelligent design in Brazil, on which he also lectures and he has signed the Dissent From Darwinism statement. He is a creationist also, and has said that evolution theory is a fallacy.(Wikipedia)

[103] Gregory J. Rummo, D.Min., M.S., M.B.A., is a Lecturer of Chemistry in the School of Arts and Sciences at Palm Beach Atlantic University and an Adjunct Scholar at the Cornwall Alliance for the Stewardship of Creation. (Minding The Campus)

Appendix I – The Predicted Demise of Evolutionary Biology

Appendix II

Scientists Reject Intelligent Design Creationism

The following is a list of scientific bodies and legislative bodies acting on scientific advice which reject Intelligent Design creationism as a valid science. It is based on a list appearing in Wikipedia. (124)

For a longer list, which includes many religious and educational bodies, see the list maintained by the National Center For Science Education – Voices for Evolution. (125)

Voices for Evolution is also the name of a book by Carrie Sager, containing the same list. A free PDF version is available from https://www.lulu.com/shop/carrie-sager/voices-for-evolution/paperback/product-3271314.html (126)

United States

Federal

American Association for the Advancement of Science.

- A 2002 statement states: "[T]he lack of scientific warrant for so-called 'intelligent design theory' makes it improper to include as a part of science education." (127)
- A 2006 statement on the teaching of evolution: "Some bills seek to discredit evolution by emphasizing so-called "flaws" in the theory of evolution or "disagreements" within the scientific community…But there is no significant controversy within the scientific community about the validity of

the theory of evolution. The current controversy surrounding the teaching of evolution is not a scientific one." (128)
- Is intelligent design a scientific alternative to contemporary evolutionary theory? No. Intelligent design proponents may use the language of science, but they do not use its methodology. They have yet to propose meaningful tests for their claims, there are no reports of current research on these hypotheses at relevant scientific society meetings, and there is no body of research on these hypotheses published in relevant scientific journals. So, intelligent design has not been demonstrated to be a scientific theory. (128)

American Association of University Professors.

AAUP membership is about 47,000, with over 500 local campus chapters and 39 state organizations.

- "…deplores efforts in local communities and by some state legislators to require teachers in public schools to treat evolution as merely a hypothesis or speculation, untested and unsubstantiated by the methods of science… These initiatives… can deny students an understanding of the overwhelming scientific consensus regarding evolution." (129)
- Regarding Academic Freedom bills: "Such efforts run counter to the overwhelming scientific consensus regarding evolution and are inconsistent with a proper understanding of the meaning of academic freedom." Cited in (130).

American Institute of Biological Sciences

Appendix II – Scientists Reject Intelligent Design Creationism

In 2015 the AIBS reaffirmed its 1972 resolution deploring the efforts by Biblical literalists to interject creationism and religion into science courses, saying:

- The theory of evolution is the only scientifically defensible explanation for the origin of life and development of species. A theory in science, such as the atomic theory in chemistry and the Newtonian and relativity theories in physics, is not a speculative hypothesis, but a coherent body of explanatory statements supported by evidence. The theory of evolution has this status. The body of knowledge that supports the theory of evolution is ever growing: fossils continue to be discovered that fill gaps in the evolutionary tree and recent DNA sequence data provide evidence that all living organisms are related to each other and to extinct species. These data, consistent with evolution, imply a common chemical and biological heritage for all living organisms and allow scientists to map branch points in the evolutionary tree.
- Biologists may disagree about the details of the history and mechanisms of evolution. Such debate is a normal, healthy, and necessary part of scientific discourse and in no way negates the theory of evolution. As a community, biologists agree that evolution occurred and that the forces driving the evolutionary process are still active today. This consensus is based on more than a century of scientific data gathering and analysis.
- Because creationism is based almost solely on religious dogma stemming from faith rather than demonstrable facts, it does not lend itself to the scientific process. As a result, creationism should not be taught in any science classroom.

- Therefore, AIBS reaffirms its 1972 resolution that explanations for the origin of life and the development of species that are not supportable on scientific grounds should not be taught as science. (131)

American Federation of Teachers.

- RESOLVED, that the American Federation of Teachers encourages and expects science teachers, in presenting evolution and other topics, to understand, respect and communicate the consensus of the scientific community in order to present the science curriculum effectively to their students; and
- RESOLVED, that the AFT will be on alert for, and opposed to, bills at the federal and state levels that attempt to use the guise of academic freedom as a means of introducing creationism, intelligent design or evolution denial into science classrooms. (130)

American Astronomical Society.

An American society of professional astronomers and other interested individuals, with over 7,000 members and six divisions.

- 2005 letter sent to President George W. Bush by society President, Dr. Robert P. Kirshner: "'Intelligent design' isn't even part of science – it is a religious idea that doesn't have a place in the science curriculum."
- 2005 statement on the Teaching of Evolution: "'Intelligent Design' fails to meet the basic definition of a scientific idea… Since 'Intelligent Design' is not science, it does not belong in the science curriculum of the nation's primary and secondary schools." (132)

Appendix II – Scientists Reject Intelligent Design Creationism

American Chemical Society

A scientific society that supports scientific inquiry in the field of chemistry, with more than 164,000 members at all degree-levels and in all fields of chemistry, chemical engineering, and related fields. It is the world's largest scientific society and one of the leading sources of authoritative scientific information.

- "…urges... State and local education authorities to support high-quality science standards and curricula that affirm evolution as the only scientifically accepted explanation for the origin and diversity of species." (133)

American Geophysical Union

The AGU represents over 43,000 Earth and space scientists.

- "Advocates of intelligent design believe that life on Earth is too complex to have evolved on its own and must therefore be the work of a designer. That is an untestable belief and, therefore, cannot qualify as a scientific theory." (134)

American Physical Society

Governing Board policy statement supporting evolution and opposing creationism.:

- The Council of the American Physical Society opposes proposals to require "equal time" for presentation in public school science classes of the biblical story of creation and the scientific theory of evolution. The issues raised by such proposals, while mainly focused on evolution, have important implications for the entire spectrum of scientific inquiry, including geology, physics, and astronomy. In contrast to "Creationism", the systematic application of scientific principles has led to a current picture of life, of the nature of our planet, and of the universe which, while incomplete, is constantly being tested and refined by observation and analysis. This ability to construct critical experiments, whose results can require rejection of a theory, is fundamental to the scientific method. ... Scientific inquiry and religious beliefs are two distinct elements of the human experience. Attempts to present them in the same context can only lead to misunderstandings of both. (135)

American Psychological Association

The Science Directorate and the APA Council of Representatives issued a Resolution Rejecting Intelligent Design As Scientific And Reaffirming Support For Evolutionary Theory.:

- Evolutionary theory is one of the most powerful elements of contemporary science. With due diligence in repudiating misappropriations of evolution to justify social injustices, scholars informed by evolutionary theory can unify scientific knowledge and serve public interests in invaluable ways. Proponents of Intelligent Design (ID) present ID theory as a viable alternative scientific explanation for the origins and diversity of life. However, ID has not withstood the scrutiny of scientific peer review of its empirical, conceptual, or epistemological bases and thus is not properly regarded as a scientific theory...
- Therefore be it resolved, that the APA reaffirms earlier relevant resolutions (APA, 1982 & 1990) and joins other leading scholarly organizations including American Association for the Advancement of Science (2002), American Astronomical Society (2005), American Society of Agronomy (2005),

Appendix II – Scientists Reject Intelligent Design Creationism

>Federation of American Societies for Experimental Biology (2005), and National Association of Biology Teachers (2005) in opposing the teaching of Intelligent Design as a scientific theory. (136)

American Society of Agronomy

The ASA represents over 10,000 members.

- Intelligent design is not a scientific discipline and should not be taught as part of the K-12 science curriculum. Intelligent design has neither the substantial research base, nor the testable hypotheses as a scientific discipline. There are at least 70 resolutions from a broad array of scientific societies and institutions that are united on this matter. As early as 2002, the Board of Directors of the American Association for the Advancement of Science (AAAS) unanimously passed a resolution critical of teaching intelligent design in public schools.
- The fundamental tenet of evolution -– descent with modification -– is accepted by the vast majority of biologists. The current debates within the research community deal with the patterns and processes of evolution, not whether the evolutionary principles presented by Darwin in 1859 hold true. These debates are similar to those surrounding the relativistic nature of gravitational waves. No one doubts the existence of gravity just because we are still learning how it works; evolution is on an equally strong footing.
- The intelligent design/creationist movement has adopted the lamentable strategy of asking our science teachers to "teach the controversy" in science curriculums, as if there were a significant debate among biologists about whether evolution underpins the abundant complexity of the biological world. We believe there is no such controversy.

- The fundamental tenet of evolution — descent with modification — is accepted by the vast majority of biologists. The current debates within the research community deal with the patterns and processes of evolution, not whether the evolutionary principles presented by Darwin in 1859 hold true. These debates are similar to those surrounding the relativistic nature of gravitational waves. No one doubts the existence of gravity just because we are still learning how it works; evolution is on an equally strong footing. (137)

American Society for Biochemistry & Molecular Biology

The ASBMB is a scientific and educational society representing 12,000 biochemists and molecular biologists.

In response to a letter published in *ASBMB Today* Professor Gregory A. Petsko, President of the society said:

- Any science teacher who teaches that evolution is controversial in a scientific sense is teaching something that is not correct and therefore is a bad teacher. The theory of evolution is as well-founded and as central to biology as atomic theory is to chemistry. Evolution is supported by both observation and experimentation. We can recapitulate it on short time scales in the laboratory with microorganisms, can watch it happen on longer time scales in the natural world (Darwin's finches being one of many examples), and can find its traces clearly laid out in the fossil record. Competing "theories" such as intelligent design have no such foundation and have been decisively rebuked as being creationism in disguise by numerous court decisions. The fact that some people don't accept a theory doesn't make it controversial scientifically. There have to be solid scientific grounds for challenging it, and there are no

Appendix II – Scientists Reject Intelligent Design Creationism

such grounds for challenging evolution. If there were, believe me, we would be the first to call for teaching them. I have no problem with teaching creationism or intelligent design in history, philosophy, or religion classes. But they, and other "challenges" to evolution, simply don't belong in a science class. (138)

- Looking back on 2009, though, the most ominous sign I see that all is not right with the world of science is the continued efforts on the part of religious fundamentalists to inject religious doctrine into the teaching of science in our public schools. Their latest ploy masquerades as "critical thinking" or "freedom of expression" and takes the form of laws prohibiting someone from being dismissed from his or her job for teaching the alleged controversy about evolution, by which they mean that it's perfectly OK for a so-called science teacher to present creationism, intelligent design and other Bible-in-science-clothing religious doctrines as legitimate alternatives to evolution, even though anyone who does so ought to be fired for incompetence. Don't be fooled: Fundamentalists have no interest in critical thinking. They do not want debates about the truth. Their intention is to replace science with religious doctrine, and I don't mean a choice of religions either. This is all about a very narrow, fundamentalist Christian point of view, one that seeks to replace evidence-based thinking with a blind faith in authority. It is very dangerous, it is not going away and it has to be fought. (139)

Botanical Society of America

- Evolution represents one of the broadest, most inclusive theories used in pursuit of and in teaching this knowledge, but it is by no means the only theory involved. Scientific theories are used in two ways: to explain what we know, and to pursue new knowledge. Evolution explains observations of shared characteristics (the result of common ancestry and descent with modification) and adaptations (the result of natural selection acting to maximize reproductive success), as well as explaining pollen:ovule ratios, weeds, deceptive pollination strategies, differences in sexual expression, dioecy, and a myriad of other biological phenomena. Far from being merely a speculative notion, as implied when someone says, "evolution is just a theory," the core concepts of evolution are well documented and well confirmed. Natural selection has been repeatedly demonstrated in both field and laboratory, and descent with modification is so well documented that scientists are justified in saying that evolution is true...

- [With creationism] No predictions are made, so there is no reason or direction for seeking further knowledge. This demonstrates the scientific uselessness of creationism. While creationism explains everything, it offers no understanding beyond, "that's the way it was created." No testable predictions can be derived from the creationist explanation. Creationism has not made a single contribution to agriculture, medicine, conservation, forestry, pathology, or any other applied area of biology. Creationism has yielded no classifications, no biogeographies, no underlying mechanisms, no unifying concepts with which to study organisms or life. In those few instances where predictions can be inferred from Biblical passages (e.g., groups of related organisms, migration of all animals from the resting place of the ark on Mt. Ararat to their present locations, genetic diversity derived from small founder populations, dispersal ability of organisms in direct proportion to their distance from eastern Turkey), creationism has been scientifically falsified.

Appendix II – Scientists Reject Intelligent Design Creationism

- Is it fair or good science education to teach about an unsuccessful, scientifically useless explanation just because it pleases people with a particular religious belief? Is it unfair to ignore scientifically useless explanations, particularly if they have played no role in the development of modern scientific concepts? Science education is about teaching valid concepts and those that led to the development of new explanations...

- The proponents of creationism/intelligent design promote scientific ignorance in the guise of learning. As professional scientists and educators, we strongly assert that such efforts are both misguided and flawed, presenting an incorrect view of science, its understandings, and its processes. (140) (CC BY-SA 3.0)

Federation of American Societies for Experimental Biology

The Federation represents 22 professional societies and 84,000 scientists...

- Supported by volumes of scientific evidence in numerous fields, evolution is among the most thoroughly tested theories in the biological sciences. The FASEB statement affirms that intelligent design and creationism are not science. These concepts fail to meet the necessary requirements for legitimate scientific theories: they are not based on direct observation or experimentation nor do they generate testable predictions. The Federation believes allowing the concepts of intelligent design and creationism into the science curricula will ultimately impair science education. (141)

- "Evolution is a critical topic to science education and is the basis for understanding biology and medicine,

> The scientific community must rise to the challenge of defending science education against initiatives that push for the teaching of creationism and intelligent design in classrooms. To not do so would be a grave disservice to our nation's students." (Bruce R. Bistrian[104].) (142)

National Association of Biology Teachers

- Scientists have firmly established evolution as an important natural process. ... Explanations or ways of knowing that invoke metaphysical, non-naturalistic or supernatural mechanisms, whether called "creation science," "scientific creationism," "intelligent design theory," "young earth theory," or similar designations, are outside the scope of science and therefore are not part of a valid science curriculum." (143)

- (Adopted by the NABT Board of Directors, 1995. Revised 1997, 2000, May 2004, and 2008. Endorsed by: The Society for the Study of Evolution, 1998; The American Association of Physical Anthropologists, 1998.)

The National Center for Science Education itself opposes the teaching of intelligent design, acting as a clearinghouse for information regarding efforts to force creationism (including intelligent design) into the classroom. The NCSE describes intelligent design as:

- a successor to the "creation science" movement, which dates back to the 1960s...The term "intelligent design" was adopted as a replacement for "creation science," which was ruled to represent a particular religious belief in the Supreme Court case Edwards v.

---

[104] FASEB President.

Aguillard in 1987. IDC proponents usually avoid explicit references to God, attempting to present a veneer of secular scientific inquiry. IDC proponents introduced some new phrases into anti-evolution rhetoric...but the basic principles behind these phrases have long histories in creationist attacks on evolution. Underlying both of these concepts, and foundational to IDC itself, is an early 19th-century British theological view, the 'argument from design.'" (144)

The NCSE also maintains lists of organizations from around the world that oppose the teaching of creationism, including intelligent design, listing 71 scientific organizations, 23 religious organizations, 43 educational organizations, and 10 civil liberties organizations.

The National Science Teachers Association NSTA.

NSTA is a professional association of 55,000 science teachers and administrators.

- We stand with the nation's leading scientific organizations and scientists, including Dr. John Marburger, the president's top science advisor, in stating that intelligent design is not science. ... It is simply not fair to present pseudoscience to students in the science classroom." (145)

The American Geophysical Union.

The union represents 43,000 Earth and space scientists.

- "Scientific theories, like evolution, relativity and plate tectonics, are based on hypotheses that have survived extensive testing and repeated verification. The President [George W. Bush] has unfortunately confused the difference between science and belief. It is essential that students understand that a scientific theory is not a belief, hunch, or untested hypothesis."

- "Ideas that are based on faith, including 'intelligent design,' operate in a different sphere and should not be confused with science. Outside the sphere of their laboratories and science classrooms, scientists and students alike may believe what they choose about the origins of life, but inside that sphere, they are bound by the scientific method." (146)

United States National Academy of Sciences, Engineering, and Medicine

The academy wrote a statement entitled "Science and Creationism: A View from the National Academy of Sciences, Second Edition National Academy of Sciences" which said that:

- "Creationism, Intelligent Design, and other claims of supernatural intervention in the origin of life or of species are not science"

- Documentation offered in support of these claims is typically limited to the special publications of their advocates. These publications do not offer hypotheses subject to change in light of new data, new interpretations, or demonstration of error. This contrasts with science, where any hypothesis or theory always remains subject to the possibility of rejection or modification in the light of new knowledge.

- No body of beliefs that has its origin in doctrinal material rather than scientific observation, interpretation, and experimentation should be admissible as science in any science course.

Appendix II – Scientists Reject Intelligent Design Creationism

> Incorporating the teaching of such doctrines into a science curriculum compromises the objectives of public education. (147)

There was also a letter from Bruce Alberts, former President, NAS:

- "We stand ready to help others in addressing the increasingly strident attempts to limit the teaching of evolution or to introduce non-scientific 'alternatives' into science courses and curricula. If this controversy arrives at your doorstep, I hope that you will both alert us to the specific issues in your state or school district and be willing to use your position and prestige as a member of the NAS in helping to work locally." (148)

State and universities

Kentucky Academy of Science

- The Kentucky Academy of Science is opposed to any attempt by legislative bodies to mandate specific content of science courses. The content of science courses should be determined by the standards of the scientific community. Science involves a continuing systematic inquiry into the manifold aspects of the biological and material world. It is abased [sic] upon testable theories which may change with new data; it cannot include interpretations based on faith or religious dogma. As scientists, we object to attempts to equate "scientific creationism" or "intelligent design" with evolution as scientific explanations of events. Teaching faith-based models implies that these views are equivalent alternatives among scientists; doing so would be misleading to students.

- "Scientific creationism" and "intelligent design" are not equivalent to evolution. There is overwhelming acceptance by scientists of all disciplines that evolution (the descent of modern specifies of animals and plants from different ancestors that lived millions of years ago) is consistent with the weight of a vast amount of evidence. The understanding of the processes underlying evolution has provided the foundation upon which many of the tremendous advances in agriculture and medicine and theoretical biology have been built. Differences among scientists over questions of how evolution was accomplished do not obscure the basic agreement that evolution has occurred. (149)

(Adopted by KAS Governing Board November 6, 1999. Passed unanimously by KAS membership November 6, 1999. Unanimously approved again at its annual business meeting on November 11, 2005. The KAS also voted to endorse the October 2002 AAAS Board Resolution on Intelligent Design Theory.)

The Kentucky Paleontological Society

Statement on Teaching Evolution states that:

- "KPS is opposed to any attempt to teach creationism or omit mention of evolution from public school instruction. Furthermore, evolution should be called "evolution" in curriculum guidelines and other documents; euphemisms such as "change over time" are intellectually dishonest for they attempt to conceal the terminology used by scientists. Paleontology relies for its evidence on two different but historically related fields, biology and geology. Biological evolution is the central organizing principle of biology, understood as descent with modification.

Evolution is equally basic to geology, because the pattern of fossil distribution in the rock record makes no sense without evolution. Evidence for the progressive replacement of fossil forms has been adequate to support the theory of evolution for over 100 years. Paleontologists may dispute, on the basis of the available evidence, the tempo and mode of evolution in a particular group at a particular time, but they do not argue about whether evolution took place. The record of the evolution of life is exciting, instructive, and enjoyable, and it is our view that everyone should have the opportunity and the privilege to understand it as paleontologists do." (Executive Committee approved this statement in 1999.) (150)

The Lehigh University Department of Biological Sciences.

Rejecting their fellow member, Michael J. Behe's claims, the Biological Science Department responded to his claims about the scientific validity and usefulness of intelligent design, publishing an official position statement which says:

Department position on evolution and "intelligent design"

- The faculty in the Department of Biological Sciences is committed to the highest standards of scientific integrity and academic function. This commitment carries with it unwavering support for academic freedom and the free exchange of ideas. It also demands the utmost respect for the scientific method, integrity in the conduct of research, and recognition that the validity of any scientific model comes only as a result of rational hypothesis testing, sound experimentation, and findings that can be replicated by others.

- The department faculty, then, are unequivocal in their support of evolutionary theory, which has its roots in the seminal work of Charles Darwin and has been supported by findings accumulated over 140 years.

- The sole dissenter from this position, Prof. Michael Behe, is a well-known proponent of "intelligent design." While we respect Prof. Behe's right to express his views, they are his alone and are in no way endorsed by the department. It is our collective position that intelligent design has no basis in science, has not been tested experimentally, and should not be regarded as scientific.

Other countries and international bodies

Elie Wiesel Foundation for Humanity

Nobel Laureates Initiative.

This organization has 38 Nobel laureates, who wrote a letter calling upon the Kansas Board of Education to reject intelligent design:

- " We, Nobel Laureates, are writing in defense of science. We reject efforts by the proponents of so-called "intelligent design" to politicize scientific inquiry and urge the Kansas State Board of Education to maintain Darwinian evolution as the sole curriculum and science standard in the State of Kansas.

- The United States has come a long way since John T. Scopes was convicted for teaching the theory of evolution 80 years ago. We are, therefore, troubled that Darwinism was described as "dangerous dogma" at one of your hearings. We are also concerned by the Board's recommendation of August 8, 2005 to allow standards that include greater criticism of evolution.

- Logically derived from confirmable evidence, evolution is understood to be the result of an unguided, unplanned process of random variation and natural selection. As the foundation of modern biology, its indispensable role has been further strengthened by the capacity to study DNA. In contrast, intelligent design is fundamentally unscientific; it cannot be tested as scientific theory because its central conclusion is based on belief in the intervention of a supernatural agent. (151)

Canadian Society for Ecology and Evolution

- There is overwhelming evidence that life has evolved over thousands of millions of years. The ancestors of modern organisms, as well as whole groups that are now completely extinct, have been found in great abundance as fossils. The main processes responsible for evolutionary change, such as variation and natural selection, have been repeatedly observed and verified in natural populations and in laboratory experiments. All the features of living organisms, including those discovered in the recent advances in molecular biology, are readily explained by the principles of evolution. Any scientific theory that provides a clear mechanism, offers a broad explanation of natural phenomena, receives strong support from observation and experiment and that is never refuted by careful investigation is usually called a "fact". The cell theory of organisms, the germ theory of infection, the gene theory of inheritance and the theory of evolution are all facts.

- Teaching alternative theories as though they had equivalent scientific status is a perversion of education that damages children's ability to understand the natural world. In particular, creationism is a religious doctrine long since known to be a fallacious account of Earth history that has no scientific standing and cannot be represented as a credible alternative to evolution.

- Evolution is the single most important principle of modern biology and the foundation of any sound biology curriculum. (152)

Council of Europe.

In 2007 the Council's "Committee on Culture, Science and Education" issued a report, *The dangers of creationism in education*, which states:

- The prime target of present-day creationists, most of whom are of the Christian or Muslim faith, is education. Creationists are bent on ensuring that their ideas are included in the school science syllabuses. Creationism cannot, however, lay claim to being a scientific discipline.

- Creationists question the scientific character of certain areas of knowledge and argue that the theory of evolution is only one interpretation among others. They accuse scientists of not providing enough evidence to establish the theory of evolution as scientifically valid. On the contrary, creationists defend their own statements as scientific. None of this stands up to objective analysis....

- There is a real risk of serious confusion being introduced into our children's minds between what

- has to do with convictions, beliefs, ideals of all sorts and what has to do with science. An "all things are equal" attitude may seem appealing and tolerant, but is in fact dangerous.
- Creationism has many contradictory aspects. The "intelligent design" idea, which is the latest, more refined version of creationism, does not deny a certain degree of evolution. However, intelligent design, presented in a more subtle way, seeks to portray its approach as scientific, and therein lies the danger....

- Creationism claims to be based on scientific rigour. In reality the methods employed by creationists are of three types: purely dogmatic assertions; distorted use of scientific quotations, sometimes illustrated with magnificent photographs; and backing from more or less well-known scientists, most of whom are not specialists in these matters. By these means creationists seek to appeal to non-specialists and spread doubt and confusion in their minds...

- The war on the theory of evolution and on its proponents most often originates in forms of religious extremism closely linked to extreme right-wing political movements. The creationist movements possess real political power. The fact of the matter, and this has been exposed on several occasions, is that some advocates of strict creationism are out to replace democracy by theocracy.

- The teaching of all phenomena concerning evolution as a fundamental scientific theory is therefore crucial to the future of our societies and our democracies. For that reason it must occupy a central position in the curriculums, and especially in the science syllabuses, as long as, like any other theory, it is able to stand up to thorough scientific scrutiny. Evolution is present everywhere, from medical overprescription of antibiotics that encourages the emergence of resistant bacteria to agricultural overuse of pesticides that causes insect mutations on which pesticides no longer have any effect. (Resolution 158) (153)

- Guillaume Lecointre[105] has shown that they have been somewhat cavalier with regard to elementary rules of science. The first breach of these rules is their lack of scepticism. In every creationist experiment, *faith imposes a preconceived idea of the expected result.* Faith does not permit them objectively to accept the result of a scientific experiment if it does not correspond to their beliefs, so it would seem impossible to reconcile faith and science. The second breach noted concerns the fact that even if the creationists seem to comply with the principles of logic, that logic is based on false premises, indeed on *a tendentious selection of facts*. Finally, mention may be made of a large number of breaches of the principles of methodological materialism and experimentation. As G. Lecointre emphasises, scientific creationism is *by definition the very opposite of science because it denies the need for recourse [...] to material realities [...] in order to establish truths.* However, let us repeat: it is not possible to establish knowledge without scientific evidence and without verifying its objectivity and scientific character by the reproduction of experiments and/or observations. The creationists make a number of claims that cannot be scientifically tested and are thus not provable. It is therefore easy to see through the deception of the creationists who claim to follow

---

[105] Guillaume Lecointre is Professor and Research Scientist at the Muséum National d'Histoire Naturelle, Paris. (Amazon author profile).

scientific principles. This deception is all the greater as, being aware that it is impossible for them to prove scientifically what their dogma advocates, some creationists even go so far as to fabricate facts and evidence. Thus, apart from the absurd interpretations put forward by some creationists, it would seem that others do not hesitate to fabricate "pseudo" evidence to try to prove the scientific nature of their statements.

- Its supporters present the Darwinian theory of evolution not as a scientific theory but as an ideology or a "natural philosophy" and therefore think it either cannot be taught in schools as a "science" or that the intelligent design ideas must be taught at the same time. There is consequently a tendency to justify the inclusion of the intelligent design ideas, which are presented as scientific because of the total lack of any reference to the Bible and God, in the school curricula. However, as G. Lecointre has shown, the intelligent design ideas are anti-science: *any activity involving blatant scientific fraud, intellectual deception or communication that blurs the nature, objectives and limits of science may be called anti-science.* The intelligent design movement would seem to be anti-science for several reasons. Firstly, *the nature of the science is distorted.* Secondly, *the objectives of the science are distorted. The writings of the leaders of this movement show that their motivations and objectives are not scientific but religious.*
- The intelligent design ideas annihilate any research process. It identifies difficulties and immediately jumps to the conclusion that the only way to resolve them is to resort to an intelligent cause without looking for other explanations. It is thus unacceptable to want to teach it in science courses. It is not enough

to present it as an alternative theory in order to have it included in the science syllabus. In order to claim to be scientific, it is only necessary to refer to *natural causes in one's explanations. The intelligent design ideas, however, only refers to supernatural causes.*(Doc. 11375. Report: Committee on Culture, Science and Education) (154)

Intelligent Design is not Science Initiative.

A coalition representing more than 70,000 Australian scientists and science teachers

This initiative was brought forth by a coalition organized by the Faculty of Science at the University of New South Wales representing more than 70,000 Australian scientists and science teachers with signatories from the Australian Academy of Science, the Federation of Australian Scientific and Technological Societies, and the Australian Science Teachers Association.

- Intelligent design is not science:

- As Australian scientists and science educators, we are gravely concerned that so-called "intelligent design" (ID) might be taught in any school as a valid scientific alternative to evolution.

- While science is a work in progress, a vast and growing body of factual knowledge supports the hypothesis that biological complexity is the result of natural processes of evolution.

- Proponents of ID assert that some living structures are so complex that they are explicable only by the agency of an imagined and unspecified "intelligent designer".

- They are free to believe and profess whatever they like. But not being able to imagine or explain how something happened other than by making a leap of faith to supernatural intervention is no basis for any science: that is a theological or philosophical notion.

- For a theory to be considered scientific it must be testable - either directly or indirectly - by experiment or observation. The results of such tests should be able to be reproduced by others as a check on their accuracy (and, importantly, if repeated testing falsifies the theory it should be rejected rather than taught as part of the accumulating body of scientific understanding).

- Finally, a scientific theory should explain more than what is already known: it should be able to predict outcomes in novel situations. Evolution meets all of these criteria but ID meets none of them: it is not science." (155)

Interacademy Panel Statement on the Teaching of Evolution.

This is a joint statement issued by the national science academies of 68 countries or international academies of science, including the United Kingdom's Royal Society, :

- We, the undersigned Academies of Sciences, have learned that in various parts of the world, within science courses taught in certain public systems of education, scientific evidence, data, and testable theories about the origins and evolution of life on Earth are being concealed, denied, or confused with theories not testable by science.

The Failure of Creationism

- We urge decision makers, teachers, and parents to educate all children about the methods and discoveries of science and to foster an understanding of the science of nature.

- Knowledge of the natural world in which they live empowers people to meet human needs and protect the planet. warning that scientific evidence about the origins of life was being "concealed, denied, or confused". It urges parents and teachers to provide children with the facts about the origins and evolution of life on Earth. (156)

The International Society for Science and Religion

- "We believe that intelligent design is neither sound science nor good theology. Although the boundaries of science are open to change, allowing supernatural explanations to count as science undercuts the very purpose of science, which is to explain the workings of nature without recourse to religious language. Attributing complexity to the interruption of natural law by a divine designer is, as some critics have claimed, a science stopper. Besides, ID has not yet opened up a new research program. In the opinion of the overwhelming majority of research biologists, it has not provided examples of "irreducible complexity" in biological evolution that could not be explained as well by normal scientifically understood processes. Students of nature once considered the vertebrate eye to be too complex to explain naturally, but subsequent research has led to the conclusion that this remarkable structure can be readily understood as a product of natural selection. This shows that what may appear to be "irreducibly complex" today may be explained naturalistically tomorrow. (157)

Appendix II – Scientists Reject Intelligent Design Creationism

Project Steve[106].

A statement signed by 1200 scientists, all named Steve.

- "Evolution is a vital, well-supported, unifying principle of the biological sciences, and the scientific evidence is overwhelmingly in favor of the idea that all living things share a common ancestry. Although there are legitimate debates about the patterns and processes of evolution, there is no serious scientific doubt that evolution occurred or that natural selection is a major mechanism in its occurrence.

- It is scientifically inappropriate and pedagogically irresponsible for creationist pseudoscience, including but not limited to "intelligent design," to be introduced into the science curricula of our nation's public schools.." (158)

The Royal Astronomical Society of Canada, Ottawa Centre.

- "The RASC Ottawa Centre supports high standards of scientific integrity, academic freedom and the free exchange of ideas. It also respects the scientific method and recognizes that the validity of any scientific model comes only as a result of rational

---

[106] NCSE's "Project Steve" is a tongue-in-cheek parody of a long-standing creationist tradition of amassing lists of "scientists who doubt evolution" or "scientists who dissent from Darwinism."… Project Steve pokes fun at this practice and, because "Steves" are only about 1% of scientists, it also makes the point that tens of thousands of scientists support evolution. And it honours the late Stephen Jay Gould, evolutionary biologist, NCSE supporter, and friend. (NCSE)

- hypotheses, sound experimentation, and findings that can be replicated by others.
- The RASC Ottawa Centre, then, is unequivocal in its support of contemporary evolutionary theory that has its roots in the seminal work of Charles Darwin and has been refined by findings accumulated over 140 years.

- Some dissenters from this position are proponents of non-scientific explanations of the nature of the universe. These may include "creation science", "creationism", "intelligent design" or other non-scientific "alternatives to evolution". While we respect the dissenters' right to express their views, these views are theirs alone and are in no way endorsed by the RASC Ottawa Centre. It is our collective position that these explanations do not meet the characteristics and rigour of scientific empiricism. (159)

The Royal Society

- The Royal Society's position is that creationism has no scientific basis and should not be part of the science curriculum. However, if a young person raises creationism in a science class, teachers should be in a position to explain why evolution is a sound scientific theory and why creationism is not, in any way, scientific." (160)

References

Appendix III

The Discovery Institute's Wedge Strategy

Prepared in 1998 and adopted thereafter, the Wedge Document lays out the strategy of the Discovery Institute to insert Christian fundamentalism into all aspects of American cultural, scientific and political life. It's declared goal is the destruction of 'Darwinism' and it's replacement by 'intelligent design' creationism.

THE WEDGE

CENTER FOR THE RENEWAL OF SCIENCE & CULTURE

INTRODUCTION

The proposition that human beings are created in the image of God is one of the bedrock principles on which Western civilization was built. Its influence can be detected in most, if not all, of the West's greatest achievements, including representative democracy, human rights, free enterprise, and progress in the arts and sciences.

Yet a little over a century ago, this cardinal idea came under wholesale attack by intellectuals drawing on the discoveries of modern science. Debunking the traditional conceptions of both God and man, thinkers such as Charles Darwin, Karl Marx, and Sigmund Freud portrayed humans not as moral and spiritual beings, but as animals or machines who inhabited a universe ruled by purely impersonal forces and whose behavior and very thoughts were dictated by the unbending forces of biology, chemistry, and environment. This materialistic conception of reality eventually infected virtually every area of our culture, from politics and economics to literature and art

The cultural consequences of this triumph of materialism were devastating. Materialists denied the existence of objective moral standards, claiming that environment dictates our behavior and beliefs. Such moral relativism was uncritically adopted by much of the social sciences, and it still undergirds much of modern economics, political science, psychology and sociology.

Materialists also undermined personal responsibility by asserting that human thoughts and behaviors are dictated by our biology and environment. The results can be seen in modern approaches to criminal justice, product liability, and welfare. In the materialist scheme of things, everyone is a victim and no one can be held accountable for his or her actions.

Finally, materialism spawned a virulent strain of utopianism. Thinking they could engineer the perfect society through the application of scientific knowledge, materialist reformers advocated coercive government programs that falsely promised to create heaven on earth.

Discovery Institute's Center for the Renewal of Science and Culture seeks nothing less than the overthrow of materialism and its cultural legacies. Bringing together leading scholars from the natural sciences and those from the humanities and social sciences, the Center explores how new developments in biology, physics and cognitive science raise serious doubts about scientific materialism and have re-opened the case for a broadly theistic understanding of nature. The Center awards fellowships for original research, holds conferences, and briefs policymakers about the opportunities for life after materialism.

The Center is directed by Discovery Senior Fellow Dr. Stephen Meyer. An Associate Professor of Philosophy at Whitworth College, Dr. Meyer holds a Ph.D. in the History and Philosophy of Science from Cambridge University. He formerly worked as a geophysicist for the Atlantic Richfield Company.

THE WEDGE STRATEGY

Phase I.
- **Scientific Research, Writing & Publicity**

Phase II.
- **Publicity & Opinion-making**

Phase III.
- **Cultural Confrontation & Renewal**

THE WEDGE PROJECTS

Phase I. Scientific Research, Writing & Publication

- Individual Research Fellowship Program
- Paleontology Research program (Dr. Paul Chien et al.)
- Molecular Biology Research Program (Dr. Douglas Axe et al.)

Phase II. Publicity & Opinion-making

- Book Publicity
- Opinion-Maker Conferences
- Apologetics Seminars
- Teacher Training Program
- Op-ed Fellow
- PBS (or other TV) Co-production
- Publicity Materials / Publications

Phase III. Cultural Confrontation & Renewal

- Academic and Scientific Challenge Conferences
- Potential Legal Action for Teacher Training
- Research Fellowship Program: shift to social sciences and humanities

FIVE YEAR STRATEGIC PLAN SUMMARY

The social consequences of materialism have been devastating. As symptoms, those consequences are certainly worth treating. However, we are convinced that in order to defeat materialism, we must cut it off at its source. That source is scientific materialism. This is precisely our strategy. If we view the predominant materialistic science as a giant tree, our strategy is intended to function as a "wedge" that, while relatively small, can split the trunk when applied at its weakest points. The very beginning of this strategy, the "thin edge of the wedge," was Phillip Johnson's critique of Darwinism begun in 1991 in *Darwinism on Trial*, and continued in *Reason in the Balance* and *Defeating Darwinism by Opening Minds*. Michael Behe's highly successful *Darwin's Black Box* followed Johnson's work. We are building on this momentum, broadening the wedge with a positive scientific alternative to materialistic scientific theories, which has come to be called the theory of intelligent design (ID). Design theory promises to reverse the stifling dominance of the materialist worldview, and to replace it with a science consonant with Christian and theistic convictions.

The Wedge strategy can be divided into three distinct but interdependent phases, which are roughly but not strictly chronological. We believe that, with adequate support, we can accomplish many of the objectives of Phases I and II in the next five years (1999-2003), and begin Phase III (See "Goals/Five Year Objectives/Activities").

Phase I: Research, Writing and Publication

Phase II: Publicity and Opinion-making

Phase III: Cultural Confrontation and Renewal

Phase I

[I]s the essential component of everything that comes afterward. Without solid scholarship, research and argument, the project would be just another attempt to indoctrinate instead of persuade. A lesson we have learned from the history of science is that it is unnecessary to outnumber the opposing establishment. Scientific revolutions are usually staged by an initially small and relatively young group of scientists who are not blinded by the prevailing prejudices and who are able to do creative work at the pressure points, that is, on those critical issues upon which whole systems of thought hinge. So, in Phase I we are supporting vital writing and research at the sites most likely to crack the materialist edifice.

Phase II.

The primary purpose of Phase II is to prepare the popular reception of our ideas. The best and truest research can languish unread and unused unless it is properly publicized. For this reason we seek to cultivate and convince influential individuals in print and broadcast media, as well as think tank leaders, scientists and academics, congressional staff, talk show hosts, college and seminary presidents and faculty, future talent and potential academic allies. Because of his long tenure in politics, journalism and public policy, Discovery President Bruce Chapman brings to the project rare knowledge and acquaintance of key op-ed writers, journalists, and political leaders. This combination of scientific and scholarly expertise and media and political connections makes the Wedge unique, and also prevents it from being "merely academic." Other activities include production of a PBS documentary on intelligent design and its implications, and popular op-ed publishing. Alongside a focus on influential opinion-makers, we also seek to build up a popular base of support among our natural constituency, namely, Christians. We will do this primarily through apologetics seminars. We intend these to encourage and equip believers with new scientific evidences that support the faith, as well as to "popularize" our ideas in the broader culture.

Phase III.

Once our research and writing have had time to mature, and the public prepared for the reception of design theory, we will move toward direct confrontation with the advocates of materialist science through challenge conferences in significant academic settings. We will also pursue possible legal assistance in response to resistance to the integration of design theory into public school science curricula. The attention, publicity, and influence of design theory should draw scientific materialists into open debate with design theorists, and we will be ready. With an added emphasis to the social sciences and humanities, we will begin to address the specific social consequences of materialism and the Darwinist theory that supports it in the sciences.

GOALS

Governing Goals

- To defeat scientific materialism and its destructive moral, cultural and political legacies.
- To replace materialistic explanations with the theistic understanding that nature and human beings are created by God.

Five Year Goals

- To see intelligent design theory as an accepted *alternative* in the sciences and scientific research being done from the perspective of design theory.
- To see the beginning of the influence of design theory in spheres other than natural science.
- To see major new debates in education, life issues, legal and personal responsibility pushed to the front of the national agenda.

Twenty Year Goals

- To see intelligent design theory as the dominant perspective in science.

- To see design theory application in specific fields, including molecular biology, biochemistry, palaeontology, physics and cosmology in the natural sciences, psychology, ethics, politics, theology and philosophy in the humanities; to see its influence in the fine arts.

- To see design theory permeate our religious, cultural, moral and political life.

Five Year Objectives

1. A major public debate between design theorists and Darwinists (by 2003)

2. Thirty published books on design and its cultural implications (sex, gender issues, medicine, law, and religion)

3. One hundred scientific, academic and technical articles by our fellows

4. Significant coverage in national media:
   - Cover story on major news magazine such as *Time* or *Newsweek*
   - PBS show such as *Nova* treating design theory fairly
   - Regular press coverage on developments in design theory
   - Favorable op-ed pieces and columns on the design movement by 3rd party media

5. Spiritual & cultural renewal:

- Mainline renewal movements begin to appropriate insights from design theory, and to repudiate theologies influenced by materialism
- Major Christian denomination(s) defend(s) traditional doctrine of creation & repudiate(s)
- Darwinism Seminaries increasingly recognize & repudiate naturalistic presuppositions
- Positive uptake in public opinion polls on issues such as sexuality, abortion and belief in God

6. Ten states begin to rectify ideological imbalance in their science curricula & include design theory

7. Scientific achievements:
    - An active design movement in Israel, the UK and other influential countries outside the US
    - Ten CRSC Fellows teaching at major universities
    - Two universities where design theory has become the dominant view
    - Design becomes a key concept in the social sciences
    - Legal reform movements base legislative proposals on design theory

ACTIVITIES

(1) Research Fellowship Program (for writing and publishing)

(2) Front line research funding at the "pressure points" (e.g., Paul Chien's Chengjiang Cambrian Fossil Find in paleontology, and Doug Axe's research laboratory in molecular biology)

(3) Teacher training

(4) Academic Conferences

(5) Opinion-maker Events & Conferences

(6) Alliance-building, recruitment of future scientists and leaders, and strategic partnerships with think tanks, social advocacy groups, educational organizations and institutions, churches, religious groups, foundations and media outlets

(7) Apologetics seminars and public speaking

(8) Op-ed and popular writing

(9) Documentaries and other media productions

(10) Academic debates

(11) Fund Raising and Development

(12) General Administrative support

References

1. **Funk, Cary & Rainie, Lee.** Chapter 4: Evolution and Perceptions of Scientific Consensus. *Pew Research Center.* [Online] Pew Research, 1 July 2015. [Cited: 12 November 2024.] https://www.pewresearch.org/internet/2015/07/01/chapter-4-evolution-and-perceptions-of-scientific-consensus/.

2. **Per Research.** Section 5: Evolution, Climate Change and Other Issues. *Pew Research Center.* [Online] Pew Research, 9 July 2009. [Cited: 12 November 2024.] https://www.pewresearch.org/politics/2009/07/09/section-5-evolution-climate-change-and-other-issues/.

3. **National Center for Science Education.** The Wedge Document. *NCSE.ngo.* [Online] National Center for Science Education, 14 October 2008. [Cited: 5 November 2024.] https://ncse.ngo/wedge-document.

4. **Various.** It is ironic that several of these individuals, who so staunchly and proudly touted their religious convictions in public, would time and again lie to cover their tracks and disguise the real purpose behind the ID Policy. *Wikipedia.* [Online] Wikipedia. [Cited: 15 November 2024.] https://en.wikipedia.org/wiki/Kitzmiller_v._Dover_Area_School_District#Potential_perjury_and_deceit.

5. **Lebo, Lauri.** *The Devil in Dover: An Insider's Story of Dogma v. Darwin in Small-Town America.* s.l. : The New Press, 2008. ISBN-13 : 978-1595582089.

6. **Talk Origins Archive.** Kitzmiller v. Dover Area School District Trial transcript: Day 12 (October 19), AM Session, Part 1. *Talk Origins Archive.* [Online] Talk Origins. [Cited: 15 November 2024.] https://www.talkorigins.org/faqs/dover/day12am.html.

7. *Simulating evolution by gene duplication of protein features that require multiple amino acid residues.* **Snoke, Michael Behe & David W.** s.l. : John Wiley & Son, 2004, Protein Science, Vol. 13. Free Access.

8. **Rubicondior, Rosa.** *The Unintelligent Designer: Refuting the Intelligent Design Hoax.* s.l. : CreateSpace Independent Publishing Platform, 2018. ISBN-13 : 978-1723144219.

9. *Substrate specificity and protein stability drive the divergence of plant-specific DNA methyltransferases.* **Jiang, Jianjun, et al.** 45, s.l. : American Association for the Advancement of Science, 6 November 2024, Science Advances, Vol. 6. Free Access.

10. *Predicting rapid adaptation in time from adaptation in space: A 30-year field experiment in marine snails.* **Castillo, Diego Garcia, et al.** 41, s.l. : American Association for the Advancement of Science, 11 October 2024, Science Advances, Vol. 10.

11. *NEAT1 promotes genome stability via m6A methylation-dependent regulation of CHD4.* **Mamontova, Victoria, et al.** s.l. : Cold Spring Harbor Laboratory Press, 3 October 2024, Genes & Development.

12. *Local cryptic diversity in salinity adaptation mechanisms in the wild outcrossing Brassica fruticulosa.* **Busoms, Silvia, et al.** 40, s.l. : PNAS, 24 September 2024, Proceedings of the National Academy of Sciences, Vol. 121, p. e2407821121.

13. **Rubicondior, Rosa.** The Teleological Fallacy or Paley's Broken Watch. *Rosa Rubicondiot.* [Online] 27 January 2012. [Cited: 22 Novermber 2024.] https://rosarubicondior.blogspot.com/2012/01/teleological-fallacy-or-paleys-broken.html.

14. *Massive horizontal gene transfer and the evolution of nematomorph-driven behavioral manipulation of mantids.*

References

Mishina, Tappei, et al. 22, s.l. : Elsevier/Cell Press, 20 November 2023, Curren Biology, Vol. 33, pp. 4988-4994.

15. *Accumulation of endosymbiont genomes in an insect autosome followed by endosymbiont replacement.* **Tvedte, Eric S., et al.** 12, s.l. : Elsevier/Cell Press, 20 June 2022, Currnr Biology, Vol. 32, pp. 2786-2795.

16. *Lateral gene transfer generates accessory genes that accumulate at different rates within a grass lineage.* **Raimondeau, P., et al.** s.l. : John Wiley & Son, 4 October 2023, New Ohytologist, Vol. 240, pp. 2072-2084.

17. *Asgard archaea defense systems and their roles in the origin of eukaryotic immunity.* **Leão, Pedro, et al.** s.l. : Springer Nature Ltd, 31 July 2024, Nature Communications, Vol. 15.

18. *Rapid large-scale evolutionary divergence in morphology and performance associated with exploitation of a different dietary resource.* **Herrel, A., et al.** 12, s.l. : American National Academy of Science, 25 March 2008, National Academy of Science of the United States of America, Vol. 105, pp. 4792-4795.

19. *TWELVE YEARS OF CONTEMPORARY ARMOR EVOLUTION IN A THREESPINE STICKLEBACK POPULATION.* **Bell, Michael A., Aguirre, Windsor E. and Buck, Nathaniel J.** s.l. : John Wiley & Sons, 2004, Evolution, Vol. 58, pp. 814-824.

20. *Adaptive differentiation following experimental island colonization in Anolis lizards.* **Losos, Jonathan B., Warheitt, Kenneth I. and Schoener, Thomas W.** s.l. : Springer Nature Ltd, 1 May 1997, Nature, Vol. 387, pp. 70–73.

21. **Darwin, Charles.** *On the Origin of Species by Means of Natural Selection or the Preservation of Favoured Races in*

the Struggle for Survival. 1st. London : John Murray, 1850. Kindle Edition.

22. *A pyritized Ordovician leanchoiliid arthropod.* **Parry, Luke A., et al.** s.l. : Elsevier Inc., 29 October 2024, Current Biology. Free access.

23. **Rubicondior, Rosa.** *Refuting Creationism: Why Creationism Fails In Both Its Science And Its Theology.* s.l. : Independently published , 2024. 979-8345104989.

24. *A nearly complete foot from Dikika, Ethiopia and its implications for the ontogeny and function of Australopithecus afarensis.* **DeSilva, Jeremy A., et al.** 7, s.l. : American association for the Advancement of Science, 4 July 2018, Science Advances, Vol. 4, p. eaar7723.

25. **Hecht, Jeff.** Almost human: closest australopithecine primate found. *New Scientist.* 8 April 2010, Vol. 328, p. 195.

26. **Bechly, Günter.** Fossil Friday: Sahelanthropus, to Be or Not to Be Bipedal. *Evolution News.* [Online] Evolution News, 9 September 1011. [Cited: 17 November 2024.] https://evolutionnews.org/2022/09/fossil-friday-sahelanthropus-to-be-or-not-to-be-bipedal/.

27. *An Ediacaran bilaterian with an ecdysozoan affinity from South Australia.* **Hughes, Ivan V., Evans, Scott D. and Droser, Mary L.** s.l. : Elsevier Inc, 18 November 2024, Current Biolog.

28. **Rubicondior, Rosa.** *What Makes You So Special?: From the Big Bang to You.* s.l. : CreateSpace Independent Publishing Platform, 2017. pp. 68-69. 978-1546788294.

29. **LePage, Michael and Lane, Nick.** How life evolved: 10 steps to the first cells. *New Scientist.* 14 October 2009.

30. *Prebiotically plausible chemoselective pantetheine synthesis in water.* **Fairchild, Jasper, et al.** 6685, s.l. :

References

American Association for the Advancement of Science, 22 February 2024, Science, Vol. 383, pp. 911-918.

31. *Aqueous microdroplets enable abiotic synthesis and chain extension of unique peptide isomers from free amino acids.* **Holden, Dylan T., Morato, Nicolás M. and Cooks, R. Graham.** 42, s.l. : National Academy of Science, 3 October 2022, Proceedings of the National Academy of Science, Vol. 119, p. e2212642119.

32. *Oxazolone mediated peptide chain extension and homochirality in aqueous microdroplets.* **Qiu, Lingqi and Cooks, R. Graham.** 2, s.l. : The National Academy of Science, 2 January 2024, Proceedings of the National Academy of Science, Vol. 121, p. e2309360120.

33. *Generation of long-chain fatty acids by hydrogen-driven bicarbonate reduction in ancient alkaline hydrothermal vents.* **Purvis, Graham, et al.** 30, s.l. : Springer Nature Ltd, 10 January 2024, Communications Earth & Environment, Vol. 5. Open access.

34. *Towards a prebiotic chemoton – nucleotide precursor synthesis driven by the autocatalytic formose reaction.* **Tran, Quoc Phuong, Yi, Ruiqin and Fahrenbach, Albert C.** . 35, s.l. : Royal Society of Chemistry, 2023, Chemical Science, Vol. 14, pp. 9589-9599.

35. **Tran, Quoc Phuong.** Did this chemical reaction create the building blocks of life on Earth? *The Conversation.* [Online] The Conversation, 14 November 2023. [Cited: 19 November 2024.] https://theconversation.com/did-this-chemical-reaction-create-the-building-blocks-of-life-on-earth-216843.

36. *Development of Allosteric Ribozymes for ATP and l-Histidine Based on the R3C Ligase Ribozyme.* **Akatsu, Yuna, Mutsuro-Aoki, Hiromi and Tamura, Koji.** 4, s.l. : MDPI (Basel, Switzerland) , 17 April 2024, Vol. 14, p. 520.

37. *RNA-catalyzed evolution of catalytic RNA.* **Papastavrou, Nikolaos, Horning, David P. and Joyce, Gerald F.** 11, s.l. : The National Academy of Science, 4 March 2024, Proceeding of the National Academy of Science, Vol. 121, p. e2321592121.

38. **Rubicondior, Rosa.** *Refuting Creationism: Why Creationism Fails In Both Its Science And Its Theology.* s.l. : Independently published , 2024. 979-8345104989.

39. *Landscape burning facilitated Aboriginal migration into Lutruwita/Tasmania 41,600 years ago.* **Adeleye, Matthew A., et al.** 46, 15 November 2024, Vol. 10.

40. **Snelling, Andrew A.** Radioisotope Dating of Rocks in the Grand Canyon. *Answers in Genesis.* [Online] Answers in Genesis, June 2005. [Cited: 21 November 2024.] https://answersingenesis.org/geology/radiometric-dating/radioisotope-dating-of-rocks-in-the-grand-canyon/.

41. **Reilly, Amanda.** Update: Creationist geologist wins permit to collect rocks in Grand Canyon after lawsuit. *Science.* [Online] American Association for the Advancement of Science., 30 June 2017. [Cited: 21 November 2024.] https://www.science.org/content/article/update-creationist-geologist-wins-permit-collect-rocks-grand-canyon-after-lawsuit.

42. **McKay, James.** Andrew Snelling's Grand Canyon rock study. *BioLogos.* [Online] BioLogos, June 2021. [Cited: 21 November 2024.] https://discourse.biologos.org/t/andrew-snellings-grand-canyon-rock-study/46213.

43. **Snelling, Andrew A.** Koongarra Uranium Deposits. [book auth.] Various. [ed.] F.E. Hughes. *Monograph 14 - Geology of the Mineral Deposits of Australia and Papua New Guinea.* Melbourne : Australasian Institute of Mining and Metallurgy, 1990, Vol. 1, 4.2, pp. 807-812.

References

44. **Alex, Dr Ritchie.** Will the Real Dr Snelling Please Stand Up? *Noansweresingenesis.* [Online] Noansweresingenesis.org. [Cited: 21 November 2024.] Previously published in The Skeptic, Vol. 11, No. 4, pp 12-15. https://www.noanswersingenesis.org.au/realsnelling.htm.

45. *The Cambrian of the Grand Canyon: Refinement of a Classic Stratigraphic Model.* **Dehler, Carol, et al.** 11, s.l. : The Geological Society of America, Inc., November 2024, GSA Today, Vol. 34, pp. 4-11.

46. *The genomic natural history of the aurochs.* **Rossi, Conor, et al.** s.l. : Springer Nature Ltd, 30 October 2024, Nature, Vol. 635, pp. 136–141.

47. *A remarkable Palaeoloxodon (Mammalia, Proboscidea) skull from the intermontane Kashmir Valley, India.* **Jukar, Advait M., et al.** s.l. : Taylor & Francis, 11 October 2024, Journal of Vertebrate Paleontology, p. e2396821.

48. *Reconstruction of human dispersal during Aurignacian on pan-European scale.* **Shao, Yaping, et al.** s.l. : Springer Nature Ltd., 28 August 2024, Vol. 15.

49. *Comparative Population Genomics of Arctic Sled Dogs Reveals a Deep and Complex History.* **Smith, Tracy A, Srikanth, Krishnamoorthy and Huson, Heather Jay.** 9, s.l. : Oxford University Press for the Society for Molecular Biology and Evolution, 28 August 2024, Genome Biology and Evolution, Vol. 16, p. evae190.

50. *Survival of mammoths (Mammuthus sp.) into the Late Pleistocene in Southwestern British Columbia (Vancouver Island), Canada.* **Termes, L. , et al.** 8, s.l. : Canadian Science Publishing, 26 July 2024, Canadian Journal of Earth Sciences, Vol. 61, pp. 843-854.

51. *Ruthenium isotopes show the Chicxulub impactor was a carbonaceous-type asteroid.* **Fischer-Gödde , Mario, et al.**

6710, s.l. : American Association for the Advancement of Science, 15 August 2024, Science, Vol. 385, pp. 752-756.

52. *Shiva and Shakti: Presumed Proto-Galactic Fragments in the Inner Milky Way.* **Malhan, Khyati and Rix, Hans-Walter** . 104, s.l. : IOP Publishing, 21 March 2024, The Astrophysical Journale, Vol. 964.

53. **Morton, G. R.** The Imminent Demise of Evolution: The Longest Running Falsehood in Creationism. *Talk Reason.* [Online] Talk Reason, 10 March 2004. [Cited: 12 Novermber 2024.] http://www.talkreason.org/articles/More.cfm.

54. **Tufts University.** The Imminent Demise of Evolution: The Longest Running Falsehood in Creationism. *Answers in Science.* [Online] Tufts University, 5 December 2021. [Cited: 12 November 2024.] https://answersinscience.org/demise.html.

55. **Penn, Granville.** *Minerals and Mosais.* London : James Duncan, 1825. p. 6. Vol. 2.

56. —. *Conversations on Geology.* London : J. W. Southgate & Sons, 1840. p. 38.

57. **Murray, John.** *Truth of Revelation: Demonstrated by an Appeal to Existing Monuments, Sculptures, Gems, Coins, and Medals,.* 2nd. London : William Smith, 1840. pp. xv-xvi. First published 1831.

58. **Miller, Hugh.** *Footsteps of the Creator.* Edinburgh : William Nimmo, 1850. p. 257.

59. **M'Farlane, Patrick.** *Antidote Against the Unscriptural and Unscientific Tendency of Modern Geology; with Remarks on Several Cognate Subjects.* London : Passmore & Alabaster, 1871. p. 89.

References

60. **Cooper, Thomas.** *Evolution, The Stone Book and The Mosaic Record of Creation.* London : Hodder & Stoughton, 1878. pp. 186-187.

61. **Dawson, J. William.** *The Meeting Place of History and Geology.* New York : Fleming H. Revell, 1894. p. 206.

62. **Wegg-Prosser, F. R.** *Dublin Review - Article VIII - Scientific Evidence of the Deluge.* Dublin : Dublin Review, 1895. p. 415.

63. **Zöckler, Professor Otto.** *The Other Side of Evolution.* 1903. pp. 31-32.

64. **Numbers, Ronal J.** *Creationism In Twentieth-Century America: A Ten-Volume Anthology of Documents, 1903-1961.* New York & London : Garland Publishing, 1995.

65. **Dennert, Eberhard.** *At The Deathbed of Darwinism.* 1904.

66. **Townsend, Luther Tracy.** *Collapse of Evolution.* Bosron and New York : National Magazine Co (Boston); American Bible League (New York), 1905.

67. **Vail, Isaac Newton.** *The Earth's Annular System.* 4th. Pasadena : The Annular Worls Co., 1912. p. v.

68. **Wright, George Frederick.** The Passing of Evolution. [book auth.] R. A. Torrey. *The Fundamentals: A Testimony to Truth.* 1941, Vol. VII, 69.

69. **Conant, Judson Eber.** *The Church, the Schools and Evolution: A Baptist Pastor Examines The Issues.* 1922. p. 18.

70. **American Association for the Advancement of Science (AAAS).** Doc id 156. [Online] 1922. http://archives.aaas.org/docs/resolutions.php?doc_id=156.

71. **Hardie, Alexander.** *Evolution: Is It Philosophical, Scientific, or Scriptural?* 1924.

72. **Clarke, Harld W.** *Back To Creationism.* 1929. p. 139.

73. **Rimmer, Harry.** *The Theory of Evolution and ht Facts of Science.* Grand Rapids : Wm. B., Eerdmans Publishing Co., 1935. pp. 113-114.

74. **Higley, L. Allen.** *Science and Truth.* London : Fleming H. Revell Co., 1940.

75. **Shute, Evan.** *Flaws in the Theory of Evolution.* New Jersey : Craig Press, 1961. p. 2.

76. **Morris, Henry M.** *The Twilight of Evolution.* Grand Rapids : Baker Book House, 1963. p. 84. ISBN-13 : 978-0932766533.

77. **Klotz, John W.** *Gene, Genesis and Evolution.* St Louis : Concordia Publishing House, 1970. p. 14. ISBN-13 : 978-1904931263.

78. **Wilson, Cliford.** *In the Beginning God.* Balston Spa, New York : Word of Truth Productions, 1975. p. 32.

79. **Gish, Duane T.** Crack in the Neo-Darwinian Jericho Part I. *Institute for Creation Research.* [Online] ICR, 1 December 1976. [Cited: 12 November 2024.] https://www.icr.org/article/crack-neo-darwinian-jericho-part-i.

80. **Morris, Henry M.** *A History of Modern Creationism.* San Diego : Master Book Publishers, 1984. pp. 329-330.

81. **Chittick, Donald E.** *The Controversy: Rootes of the Creation-Evolution Conflict.* s.l. : Creation Compas, 1984. p. 191.

82. **Ankerberg, John.** *The John Ankerberg Show.* 1987.

83. **Southerland, Luther D.** *Darwin's Enigma.* Santee, California : Master Books, 1988. pp. 7,8.

References

84. *Natural selection and the emergence of mind.* . **Popper, Karl.** 1978, Dialectica, Vol. 32, pp. 339-355.

85. **Morris, Henry M.** Evolution - A House Divided. *Institute for Creation Research.* [Online] ICR, 1 August 1989. [Cited: 12 Novermber 2024.] https://www.icr.org/article/evolution-house-divided.

86. **Looy, Mark.** "I Think, Therefore There Is a Supreme Thinker". *Answers in Genesis.* [Online] AiG, 1 October 1990. [Cited: 12 Novermber 2024.] https://www.icr.org/article/335/206/.

87. **Gish, Duane T.** The Big Bang Theory Collapses" Impact. *Institute for Creation Research.* [Online] IcR, 1 June 1991. [Cited: 12 Novermber 2024.] https://www.icr.org/article/big-bang-theory-collapses/.

88. **Kenyon, Percival Davis & Dean H.** *Of Pandas and People.* Dallas : Haughton Publishing Co., 1993. pp. 64,67.

89. **Varughese, T. V.** Christianity and Technological Advance - The Astonishing Connection. *Institute for Creation Research.* [Online] ICR, 1 November 1993. [Cited: 12 Novermber 2024.] https://www.icr.org/article/christianity-technological-advance-astonishing-con.

90. **Morris, John D.** *The Young Earth.* Colorado Springs : Master Books, 1994. p. 121.

91. **Boys, Don.** *Evolution, Fact, Fraud or Faith.* Largo, FL : Freedom Publications, 1994. pp. 44-45.

92. **Morris, Henry M.** Cosmology's Holy Grail. *Institute for Creation Research.* [Online] ICR, 1 February 1995. [Cited: 12 Novermber 2024.] https://www.icr.org/article/cosmologys-holy-grail.

93. **Johnson, Phillip E.** What (If Anything) Hath God Wrought? Academic Freedom and the Religious Professor.

leaderu.com. [Online] 1995. [Cited: 13 November 2024.] https://www.leaderu.com/pjohnson/wrought.html.

94. **Ross, Hugh.** *Beyond the Cosmos.* Colorado Springs : NavPress, 1996. p. 33.

95. **Johnson, Phillip E.** The Soryteller and the Scientist. *First Things.* [Online] First Things, October 1996. [Cited: 13 November 2024.] https://www.firstthings.com/article/1996/10/001-the-storyteller-and-the-scientist.

96. **Buckna, David.** Evolution: Its Collapse In View? *Revolution Against Evolution.* [Online] RAE, 2 February 1997. [Cited: 13 November 2024.] https://www.rae.org/wp-content/uploads/2017/03/collapse.pdf.

97. **Dembski, William A.** Introduction. [book auth.] William A. Dembski, et al. *Mere Creationism.* Downer's Grove, IL : Intervarsity Press: Academic, 1998.

98. —. Redesigning Science. [book auth.] William A. Dembski, et al. *Mere Creationism.* Downer's Grove IL : Invervarsity Press, 1998, pp. 93-112, 93.

99. **Johnson, Phillip E.** How to Sink a Battleship. [book auth.] William A. Dembski, et al. [ed.] William A. Dembski. *Mere Creation.* Downer's Grove IL : Intervarsity Press, 1998, pp. 446-453, 453.

100. **Reardon, Patrick Henry.** The Word as Text. *Touchstone.* [Online] Touchstone, 1999. [Cited: 13 November 2024.] https://www.touchstonemag.com/archives/article.php?id=12-04-085-f.

101. **Bolin, Roy.** The Natural Limits to Biological Change. [book auth.] Various. [ed.] Ray Bolin. *Creation, Evolution & Modern Science.* Grand Rapids : Kregel Publications, 2000, p. 44.

References

102. **Morris, Henry M.** The Scientific Case Against Evolution: A Summary, Part II. *Institute for Creation Research.* [Online] ICR, 2001. 13 Novermber 2024 the articles appears to have been taken down, but is still widely cited in the creationist literature..

103. **Brewer, Gregory J.** The Imminent Death of Darwinism and the Rise of Intelligent Design. *Institute for Creation Research.* [Online] ICR, 10 November 2001. [Cited: 13 November 2024.] https://www.icr.org/article/imminent-death-darwinism-rise-intelligent-design/.

104. **Morris, Henry M.** What are They Afraid Of? *Institute for Creation Research.* [Online] ICR, 1 December 2001. [Cited: 13 November 2024.] https://www.icr.org/article/542.

105. **Muncaster, Ralph O.** *Why Are Scientists Turnign to God?* Eugene, ORHarvest House Publishers : s.n., 2002. pp. 19,21,35.

106. **Muncaster, Ralps O.** *Dismantling Evolution.* Eugene. OR : Harvest House Publishers, 2003. p. 56.

107. **Schaefer, Henry F.** *Science and Chriatianity: Conflict or Coherence?* Watkinsville GA : The Appollo Trust, 2003. p. 96.

108. **Jeffrey, Grant R.** *Creation: Remarkable Evidence of God's Design.* Toronto : Frontier Research Publications, 2003. pp. 168, 174.

109. **Ross, Fazale Rana & Hugh.** *Origins of Life.* Colorado Springs : NavPress, 2004. p. 27.

110. **Dembski, William A.** *The Designer Revolution.* Downer's Grove IL : InterVarsity Press, 2004. pp. 28, 50.

111. —. The Measure of Design: A Conversation About the Past, Present & Future of Darwinism & Design. *Toutchstone.* [Online] Mere Christianity, 2004. [Cited: 13 November 2024.]

https://www.touchstonemag.com/archives/article.php?id=17-06-060-i.

112. **Johnson, Phillip E.** worldmag.com. *World.* [Online] Worldmag, 4 April 2004. Offline when checked 13 November 2024. http://www.worldmag.com/world/issue/04-03-04/cover_2.asp.

113. **Wells, Jonathan.** Whatever Happened to Evolution. *World Magazine.* [Online] worldmag, 3 April 2004. Offline 13 November 2024.

114. **R. Albert Mohler, Jr.** Editorial. *Christian Post.* [Online] Christian Post, 2004. Appears to have been taken down 13 November 2024. http://www.christianpost.com/dbase/editorial/203|8|14|21|28/4.htm.

115. **National Council for Science Education.** Monkey see, monkey do? *NCSE.* [Online] National Council for Science Education, 27 May 2005. [Cited: 13 November 2024.] https://ncse.ngo/monkey-see-monkey-do.

116. **Christian Post.** Intelligent Design Supporters Say Theory in 'Infancy'. *Christian Post.* [Online] Christian Post, 2006. [Cited: 13 November 2024.] Citing AP. https://www.christianpost.com/news/intelligent-design-supporters-say-theory-in-infancy.html.

117. **O'Leary, Denyse.** What I would Tell the Catholic Church re Intelligent design and evolution. *Theologyweb.* [Online] Theologyweb, 29 August 2006. Unreachable - 13 November 2024. http://www.theologyweb.com/campus/private.php?do=showpm&pmid=230270.

118. **Kwon, Lillian.** Science Gives Christians Upper Hand Over Atheists. *The Christian Post.* [Online] The Christian Post, 18 November 2006. [Cited: 13 November 2024.]

References

Quoting Jay Richards.
https://www.christianpost.com/article/20061118/23538.htm.

119. **Fodor, Jerry.** Why Pigs Don't Have Wings. *London Review of Books.* [Online] London Review of Books, 18` October 2007. [Cited: 13 November 2024.] https://www.lrb.co.uk/the-paper/v29/n20/jerry-fodor/why-pigs-don-t-have-wings.

120. **Fuller, Steve.** *Science vs Religion? Intelligent Design and the Problem of Evolution.* Cambridge : Polity Press, 2007. p. 126.

121. **Arrington, Barry.** What's New At UD. *Uncommon Descent.* [Online] Uncommon Descent, 14 November 2008. [Cited: 13 November 2024.] https://uncommondescent.com/intelligent-design/whats-new-at-ud/.

122. **Eberlin, Marcus.** Game of Thrones: As Darwinism Dissolves, Top Evolutionists Scramble for a Successor. *Evolution News.* [Online] Evolution News, 22 May 2019. [Cited: 13 November 2024.] https://evolutionnews.org/2019/05/game-of-thrones-as-darwinism-dissolves-top-evolutionists-scramble-for-a-successor/.

123. **Rummo, Gregory J.** A Short Reminder: Intelligent Design Is Winning the Origins Debate. *Minding The Camous).* [Online] Minding the Campus, Inc., 11 October 2024. [Cited: 13 November 2024.] https://www.mindingthecampus.org/2024/10/11/a-short-reminder-intelligent-design-is-winning-the-origins-debate/.

124. **Various.** List of scientific bodies explicitly rejecting intelligent design. *Wikipedia* . [Online] Wikipedia, 29 August 2023. [Cited: 13 November 2024.] https://en.wikipedia.org/wiki/List_of_scientific_bodies_explicitly_rejecting_intelligent_design.

125. **National Center For Science Education.** Voices for Evolution. *National Center For Science Education.* [Online] NCSE, February 29 2016. [Cited: 15 November 2024.] https://ncse.ngo/voices-evolution-0.

126. **Sager, Carrie.** *Voices for Evolution.* 2007. 9780615204611.

127. **American Association for the Advancement of Science.** AAAS Board Resolution on Intelligent Design Theory. *AAAS.* [Online] American Association for the Advancement of Science, 1 July 2013. [Cited: 14 November 2024.] https://www.aaas.org/news/aaas-board-resolution-intelligent-design-theory.

128. —. Statement on the Teaching of Evolution. *AAAS.* [Online] American Association for the Advancement of Science, 16 February 2006. [Cited: 14 November 2024.] PDF. https://www.aaas.org/sites/default/files/0219boardstatement.pdf.

129. **American Association of University Professors.** National Center For Science Education. *American Association of University Professors.* [Online] NCSE, 24 November 2008. [Cited: 14 November 2024.] https://ncse.ngo/american-association-university-professors.

130. **American Federation of Teachers.** AGAINST SO-CALLED ACADEMIC FREEDOM BILLS THAT UNDERMINE THE ACCURATE TEACHING OF EVOLUTION. *American Federation of Teachers.* [Online] AFT. [Cited: 14 November 2024.] https://www.aft.org/resolution/against-so-called-academic-freedom-bills-undermine-accurate-teaching-evolution.

131. **American Institute of Biological Sciences.** American Institute of Biological Sciences. *National Center For Science Education.* [Online] NCSE, 16 December 2015. [Cited: 15

References

November 2024.] https://ncse.ngo/american-institute-biological-sciences.

132. **Kirshner, Robert P.** And Now A Word From the Astronomers.... *National Geographic.* [Online] National Geographic, 5 August 2005. [Cited: 14 November 2024.] https://www.nationalgeographic.com/science/article/and-now-a-word-from-the-astronomers.

133. **National Center for Science Education.** ACS issues statement on teaching evolution. *National Center for Science Education.* [Online] NCSE, 22 June 2005. [Cited: 14 November 2004.] https://ncse.ngo/acs-issues-statement-teaching-evolution.

134. **Zimmer, Carl.** 43,000 Scientists: Bush Puts Schoolchildren At Risk. *National Geographic.* [Online] National Geographic, 2 August 2005. [Cited: 14 November 2024.] https://www.nationalgeographic.com/science/article/43000-scientists-bush-puts-schoolchildren-at-risk.

135. **American Physical Society.** APS Statement on Creationism. *APS125.* [Online] APS. [Cited: 14 November 2024.] https://www.aps.org/archives/publications/apsnews/199911/statement.cfm.

136. **American Psychological Ossociation.** APA Council of Representatives Resolution Rejecting Intelligent Design as Scientific and Reaffirming Support for Evolutionary Theory. *American Psychological Ossociation.* [Online] American Psychological Ossociation, 9 February 2007. [Cited: 14 November 2024.] https://www.apa.org/about/policy/intelligent-design.

137. **American Society of Agronomy.** Scientific societies support teaching evolution. *Eureka Alert.* [Online] AAAS, 15

August 2005. [Cited: 14 November 2024.] https://www.eurekalert.org/news-releases/690960.

138. **Petsko, Gregory A.** ASBM Today. *New Orleans Welcomes ASMB.* [Online] American Society for Biochemistry and Molecular Biology, April 2009. [Cited: 14 November 2024.] PDF. https://www.asbmb.org/Asbmb.Web/media/files/atoday/ASBMBToday-2009-04.pdf.

139. —. Ring in the New. *ASBMB Today.* [Online] American Society for Biochemistry and Molecular Biology, 2010. [Cited: 14 November 2024.] Wayback Macine. https://web.archive.org/web/20170402083408/https://www.asbmb.org/asbmbtoday/asbmbtoday_article.aspx?id=4904&terms=intelligent%20design.

140. **Botanical Society of America.** Botanical Society of America's Statement on Evolution. *Botanical Society of America.* [Online] Botanical Society of America. [Cited: 14 November 2024.] https://botany.org/home/resources/botanical-society-of-americas-statement-on-evolution.html.

141. **Federation of American Societies for Experimental Biology.** FASEB oposes using science classes to teach intelligent design, creationism and other nonscientific beliefs. *FASEB Journal.* [Online] Federation of American Societies for Experimental Biology, March 2006. [Cited: 14 November 2024.] PDF (read only). https://faseb.onlinelibrary.wiley.com/doi/epdf/10.1096/fj.06-0302ufm.

142. **Bistram, Bruce R.** FASEB oposes using science classes to teach intelligent design, creationism and other non-scientific beliefs. *FASB Journal.* [Online] Federation of American Societies for Experimental Biology, March 2006. [Cited: 14 Novermber 2024.] PDF (Read only).

References

https://faseb.onlinelibrary.wiley.com/doi/epdf/10.1096/fj.06-0302ufm.

143. **National Association of Biology Teachers.** National Association of Biology Teachers (2008). *National Center For Science Education.* [Online] NCSE, 2008. [Cited: 14 November 2024.] https://ncse.ngo/national-association-biology-teachers-2008.

144. **National Center For Science Education.** What is "Intelligent Design" Creationism? *National Center For Science Education.* [Online] NCSE, 17 October 2008. [Cited: 14 November 2024.] https://ncse.ngo/what-intelligent-design-creationism.

145. **Cartwright, Reed A.** Statement on ID Education. *Panda's Thumb.* [Online] Panda's Thumb, 4 August 2005. [Cited: 14 November 2024.] https://pandasthumb.org/archives/2005/08/statements-on-i.html.

146. **Spilhaus, Fred (cited by Cartwright, Reed A.).** Statement on ID in Education. *Panda's Thumb.* [Online] Panda's Thumb, 4 August 2005. [Cited: 14 November 2024.] https://pandasthumb.org/archives/2005/08/statements-on-i.html.

147. **National Academies of Sciences, Engineering, and Medicine.** Science and Creationism. *National Academies of Sciences, Engineering, and Medicine.* [Online] National Academies of Sciences, Engineering, and Medicine., 1999. [Cited: 14 November 2024.] https://nap.nationalacademies.org/catalog/6024/science-and-creationism-a-view-from-the-national-academy-of.

148. **Leith, Audrey.** NAS President Urges Support for Teaching of Evolution. *FYI: Science Policy News.* [Online] American Institute of Physics (AIP), 6 April 2006. [Cited: 14

November 2024.] https://ww2.aip.org/fyi/2005/nas-president-urges-support-teaching-evolution.

149. **Kentucky Academy of Sciences (KAS)**. KAS Members Approve Resolution in Support of Evolution Press Release: December 22, 2005. *Wayback Machine.* [Online] KAS, 2005. [Cited: 14` November 2024.] https://web.archive.org/web/20070929082324/http://www.kyacademyofscience.org/news/evolution.html.

150. **KENTUCKY PALEONTOLOGICAL SOCIETY (KPS).** KENTUCKY PALEONTOLOGICAL SOCIETY STATEMENT ON THE TEACHING OF EVOLUTION. *KENTUCKY PALEONTOLOGICAL SOCIETY.* [Online] KPS, 12 October 1999. [Cited: 14 November 2024.] https://www.uky.edu/OtherOrgs/KPS/pages/evolution.html.

151. **Nobel Laureates.** A Letter from Nobel Laureates. *Live Journal.* [Online] THE ELIE WIESEL FOUNDATION FOR HUMANITY, 9 September 2005. [Cited: 14 November 2024.] https://endcreationism.livejournal.com/78223.html.

152. **Canadian Society for Ecology and Evolution.** Canadian Society for Ecology and Evolution. *National Center For Science Education.* [Online] NCSE, 16 December 2015. [Cited: 15 November 2024.] https://ncse.ngo/canadian-society-ecology-and-evolution.

153. **Parliamentary Assembly (Council of Europe).** Resolution 158 (2007) The dangers of creationism in education. *The Council of Europe.* [Online] The Cuncil of Europe, 2007. [Cited: 14 November 2024.] https://assembly.coe.int/nw/xml/XRef/Xref-XML2HTML-EN.asp?fileid=17592&lang=en.

154. **Committee on Culture, Science and Education (Rapporteur: Mrs Anne BRASSEUR, Luxembourg, ALDE).** The dangers of creationism in education. *Council of Europe.* [Online] Council of Europe, 17 September 2007.

References

[Cited: 14 November 2024.] https://assembly.coe.int/nw/xml/XRef/X2H-Xref-ViewHTML.asp?FileID=11751&lang=EN.

155. **UNSW Faculty of Science.** INTELLIGENT DESIGN IS NOT SCIENCE. *Wayback Machine.* [Online] UNSW Faculty of Medicine, 2005. [Cited: 14 November 2024.] https://web.archive.org/web/20070811105349/http://www.science.unsw.edu.au/news/2005/intelligent.html.

156. **The Interacademy Panel (IAP).** IAP STATEMENT ON THE TEACHING OF EVOLUTION. *The Interacdemy Panel on International Issues.* [Online] IAP. [Cited: 14 November 2024.] PDF. https://www.interacademies.org/sites/default/files/2020-05/Evolution%20statement.pdf.

157. **The International Society for Science and Religion.** ISSR Staement: The Concept of 'Intelligent Design'. *The International Society for Science and Religion.* [Online] ISSR. [Cited: 14 November 2024.] https://www.issr.org.uk/issr-statements/concept-intelligent-design/.

158. **National Center For Science Education, .** Project Steve. *Project Steve.* [Online] NCSE, 7 March 2016. [Cited: 14 November 2024.] https://ncse.ngo/project-steve.

159. **Royal Astronomical Society of Canada – Ottawa Centre.** A Position Statement of the Royal Astronomical Society of Canada – Ottawa Centre on Science & Evolution. *Crater Explorer.* [Online] Ottawa Centre -RASC, 26 April 2007. [Cited: 14 November 2024.] https://craterexplorer.ca/ottawa-centre-rasc-position-statement/.

160. **The Royal Society.** Royal Society statement regarding Professor Michael Reiss. *News From The Royal Society.* [Online] The Royal Society, 16 September 2008. [Cited: 14

November 24.] https://royalsociety.org/news/2012/professor-michael-reiss/.

Index

^{14}C	90, 91, 113
^{16}O	92, 109
^{18}O	92, 109
Abiogenesis	6, 68, 75, 77, 79, 84, 154
Abric Pizarro	107, 108
Active information	35
Adeleye, Dr Matthew	89
Adenine	85
African ape	62
Alberts, Bruce	175
Allele frequency	23, 47, 54, 55
Allopatric speciation	31
American Association for the Advancement of Science	4, 5, 134, 135, 161, 167
American Association of University Professors	162
American Astronomical Society	164, 167
American Chemical Society	165
American Federation of Teachers	164
American Geophysical Union	165, 173
American Institute of Biological Sciences	163
American Physical Society	165
American Psychological Association	166
American Society for Biochemistry & Molecular Biology	168
American Society of Agronomy	167
Amino acid	10, 16, 26, 39, 42, 71, 74, 75, 76, 80, 83, 84, 85, 86, 148
Angular momentum	117
Anolis sagrei	54
Answers in Genesis	93, 94, 144
AnswersInScience	126
Arabidopsis thaliana	15, 16
Argonautes	46
Argument from complexity	14
Arms races	46
Arrington, Barry	158
Arthropod evolution	60

Asgard archaea 21, 46, 47
Astronomy 146, 166
Ataxia Telangiectasia Mutated 26
Aurignacian 102
Auroch 98, 99, 106
Australian Academy of Science 184
Australian Science Teachers Association 184
Australian scientists 184
Australopithecine 61, 62, 63
Australopithecus 61, 62, 63
　afarensis 61
　sediba 62
Barriers to hybridization 31
Bdelloid rotifers 41
Bearing false witness 7
Beecher's Bed 57, 58
Behe, Michael J. 4, 7, 8, 10, 13, 14, 87, 147, 177, 178, 193
Berlinski, David 125, 148
Bible 18, 87, 88, 95, 98, 105, 106, 111, 113, 115, 117, 121,
　126, 127, 133, 137, 146, 152, 154, 183, 237
Bible-in-science-clothing 169
Biblical creation 151
Big Bang 5, 6, 70, 84, 115, 122, 144, 145, 146, 238
　cosmologies 144
Biochemistry 7, 196
Biological sciences 171, 187
Biology 16, 18, 20, 134, 136, 153, 154, 155, 168, 170, 171,
　176, 179, 180, 189, 190, 196, 197
Bistrian, Bruce R. 172
Blatant scientific fraud 183
Bohlin, Ray 151
Botanical Society of America 169
Brachiopod 96, 97
Brahma 118
Brassica
　fruticulose 30
　napus 30
　oleracea 30
BRCA1 mutations 28

Index

BRCA2 mutations 28
Brewer, Gregory J. 152
Bright Angel Shale 96
British Museum of Natural History 142
Bronze Age 84, 105, 106, 111, 112, 115
Buckna, David 149
Bush, President George W. 11, 164, 173
Caecal valves 51
Cambrian 58, 60, 61, 65, 66, 67, 96, 97, 122, 197
Campbell, John Angus 11
Canadian Society for Ecology and Evolution 179
Cancer 19, 27, 28, 29
Cell theory of organisms 179
Center for Reclaiming America for Christ 141
Center for Science and Culture 7, 8, 125, 147
Center for the Renewal of Science and Culture 151, 190
Chapman, Bruce 11, 194
Charniodiscus 67
Chemistry 36, 163, 165, 168, 189
Chimpanzee 61, 62, 64
Chittick, Dr. Donald E. 141
Christian 8, 9, 14, 18, 93, 125, 126, 128, 138, 139, 141, 145, 148, 150, 152, 153, 154, 180, 189, 193, 194, 197
Christian fundamentalism 8, 126, 189
Christian fundamentalist 9, 121
Christian god 14, 18
Clark, Harold Willard 136
Common designer 45, 46, 59
Complex molecular structures 155
Complex specificity 35
Complexity 8, 13, 14, 17, 18, 25, 26, 29, 32, 34, 35, 44, 46, 149, 168, 184, 186
Conditional probabilities 35
Convergent evolution 38
Cooks, Professor R. Graham 75
Cooper, Thomas 130
Copper Age 112
Cosmology 196
Council of Europe 180

Creation science movement 172
Creation Week 88, 136
'Creation Week 88, 89, 113, 115
Creationism1, 6, 7, 8, 9, 11, 18, 19, 20, 22, 31, 48, 59, 84, 87,
    90, 104, 110, 123, 124, 125, 130, 131, 136, 137, 140, 142,
    149, 152, 154, 161, 163, 164, 165, 166, 168, 169, 170, 171,
    172, 173, 174, 175, 176, 180, 181, 188, 189, 238
    dangers of in education 180
Creationist6, 8, 9, 13, 14, 15, 18, 21, 23, 24, 26, 36, 43, 44, 45,
    47, 48, 49, 54, 55, 56, 57, 59, 61, 62, 63, 66, 68, 69, 73, 79,
    84, 89, 93, 94, 96, 98, 99, 100, 104, 105, 106, 125, 126,
    133, 134, 137, 138, 139, 140, 141, 144, 145, 148, 149, 152,
    153, 159, 167, 170, 173, 180, 181, 182, 183, 187, 239
    dogma 121
    groups 55
    literature 55
Cretaceous-Paleogene boundary 114, 115
Cytosine 16, 32, 85
Darwin, Charles4, 8, 11, 18, 33, 49, 56, 57, 59, 126, 129, 130,
    140, 142, 147, 148, 149, 151, 154, 156, 158, 167, 168, 178,
    188, 189, 193
Darwin's Black Box 4, 11
Darwinian
    evolution 18, 36, 80, 81, 144, 145, 152, 155, 178
    molecular evolution 4
    processes 155
    theory 157, 183
Darwinism8, 24, 51, 56, 125, 131, 135, 147, 148, 152, 155,
    156, 157, 158, 159, 178, 187, 189, 193, 197
Darwinist 142, 154, 158, 195, 196
Davis, Percival William 144
Dawson, Sir John William 130
Dehler, Professor Carol 97
Dembski, William A.8, 11, 31, 32, 33, 34, 36, 37, 38, 44, 45,
    87, 121, 125, 147, 149, 155, 157, 158
Denisovans 63, 100
Dennert, Eberhard 132
Descent with modification 6, 39, 167, 168, 170, 176
Design theory 161, 172, 194, 195, 196, 197

Index

Dickinsonia 67
Digital Sky Survey 117
Dinosaurs 87, 113, 122
Discovery Institute 6, 7, 8, 10, 11, 15, 18, 31, 38, 87, 121, 125, 143, 147, 149, 151, 189, 190
Disinformation campaign 61
DNA 15, 16, 17, 19, 20, 25, 26, 27, 28, 29, 32, 36, 38, 39, 46, 55, 71, 75, 78, 79, 81, 84, 85, 113, 151, 163, 179
    damage 26, 27, 28
    junk 38
    Junk 26
    mitochondrial 50, 99
    Neanderthal 102
    repair 28
    replication 16, 27
    sequence 27
Doppler effect 116
Droser, Professor Mary 65
Drosophila ananassae 42
Durga 118
Eberlin, Marcos 159
Economics 190
Ediacara Member 66, 67
Ediacaran
    biota 67
    Period 65, 66
Edwards v. Aguillard 172
Elephas
    maximus 101
Elie Wiesel Foundation for Humanity 178
Endogenous retroviruses 39, 40
Endosymbiosis 46
Environment 19, 22, 23, 33, 36, 37, 38, 41, 45, 50, 52, 53, 58, 189, 190
Epigenetic 16, 17, 18, 19, 20, 29
Epigenetic system 17, 18
Establishment Clause 125, 143
Ethics 196
Eukaryote 21, 33, 41, 46, 47

225

European Committee on Culture, Science and Education 180, 184
European Space Agency 116
Evangelical Christians 87
Evangelism Explosion International 141
Evolution 4, 7, 14, 17, 18, 20, 21, 23, 30, 33, 37, 40, 42, 45, 46, 47, 48, 54, 55, 62, 63, 65, 123, 125, 130, 131, 132, 133, 134, 135, 136, 137, 138, 139, 140, 141, 142, 143, 144, 145, 148, 149, 151, 152, 153, 154, 155, 156, 158, 159, 161, 162, 163, 164, 165, 166, 167, 168, 169, 170, 171, 172, 173, 175, 176, 177, 178, 179, 180, 181, 184, 185, 186, 187, 188
  goal-seeking 45
Evolutionary
  biologist 147, 148, 187
  biology 20, 24, 45, 58, 69, 125, 147, 155
  process 47, 56, 71, 81, 163
  science 147
Evolutionist 21, 137, 140, 151, 152, 156, 158
Fahrenbach, Albert C. 78
False dichotomy 8, 13, 32, 85, 238
False equivalence fallacy 33
False witnessing 121
Federation of American Societies for Experimental Biology
  .... 167, 171
Federation of Australian Scientific and Technological
  Societies 184
Fine art 196
Flagellar motor 25
Fodor, Jerry Allen 157
Foraminifera 92, 109, 110
Fossilisation process 56, 57
Freud, Sigmund 189
Fruit flies 21
Fuller, Steve William 158
Functional complexity 35, 121
Fundamentalist 7, 18, 117, 137, 143, 151, 169, 237
Fundamentalist Christian 18, 169
Fundamentalist theocracy 143
Futuyma, Douglas Joel 147

Index

Ganesha 118
Gasterosteus aculeatus..52
Gene duplication 15, 16
Gene pool 14, 33, 35, 38, 47
Gene theory of inheritance 179
Genes15, 16, 19, 26, 27, 37, 38, 39, 40, 41, 44, 64, 81, 99, 101, 122
    jumping..15
Genesis 18, 116, 130, 149
Genetic
    bottleneck 99
    code 38, 84, 85, 86, 145
    diversity 40, 41, 63, 64, 170
    drift 6, 24
    evidence...151
    information 15, 26, 27, 31, 32, 34, 38, 40, 80
    isolation 63
    messages...144
Genocidal flood 93, 111, 115, 122
Genome15, 17, 19, 20, 23, 25, 31, 32, 36, 37, 39, 40, 42, 44, 45, 64
Genomic instability 28
Geochronological methods....................................59
Geological column 23
Geology 127, 128, 134, 135, 166, 176, 177
Germ theory of infection 179
Gish, Duane Tolbert 140, 143, 144
Global genocidal flood 87, 102, 104
Goal-orientated..35
Goal-seeking process..36, 45
God did it! 31
God of the gaps 8, 13, 32
Gorilla...62
Gould, Stephen Jay..................................148, 187
Grand Canyon 93, 96, 97
Great Cambrian Transgression..............................97
Guanine 16, 32, 85
Ham, Ken 144
Hammerhead ribozyme 81, 82

Heath-Robinson, William ... 24, 25, 29
Hebrew mythology ... 111
Higley, Louis Allen ... 137
Hindu
    deities ... 117
    mythology ... 117
    philosophy ... 118
    religious thought ... 119
    scriptures ... 118, 119
    texts ... 118, 119, 120
    tradition ... 117
    trinity ... 118
Hinduism ... 118, 119
Historical processes ... 126
Hominin ... 62, 63, 64, 100, 101
Homo ... 61, 62, 63, 64
    erectus ... 63, 100, 148, 149
    sapiens ... 62, 63, 102, 148, 149
Horizontal gene transfer ... 36, 38, 39, 40, 42
Horning, David ... 81
Horseshoe crabs ... 57, 66
Hoyle, Fred ... 145
Hughes, Ian ... 66
Humanities ... 190, 192, 195, 196
Huttonism ... 128
iFne-tuned Universe fallacy ... 85
Ignorant incredulity ... 84, 238
Incompetence ... 20, 169
Institute for Creation Research ... 138, 140, 145, 152
Intellectual deception ... 183
Intelligent design 4, 6, 7, 8, 10, 11, 13, 14, 15, 17, 19, 20, 21, 23, 25, 28, 31, 51, 89, 121, 125, 126, 144, 147, 149, 151, 152, 155, 156, 157, 158, 159, 161, 162, 164, 165, 166, 167, 168, 169, 171, 172, 173, 174, 175, 176, 177, 178, 179, 181, 183, 184, 185, 186, 187, 188, 189, 193, 194
    creationism ... 6, 31, 87, 121, 151, 161
    creationists ... 17, 23, 24, 25, 28, 47
    movement ... 144, 147, 156
    theory ... 159, 176, 195

Index

Intelligent Design is not Science Initiative 184
Intelligent designer 14, 19, 23, 25, 29, 184
Intelligently designed 25, 26, 28, 29
Interacademy Panel Statement on the Teaching of Evolution
.... 185
Intermediate form 57
Irreducible complexity 8, 10, 11, 29, 186
Johnson, Phillip E. 147, 150, 155, 193
Jones, Judge John E. III 11
Joyce, Gerald 81
Jukar, Advait 100
Kali 118
Kartikeya 118
Kennedy, Dennis James 141
Kentucky Academy of Science 175
Kenyon, Dean H. 144
Kirshner, Dr. Robert P. 164
Kitzmiller vs. Dover 4, 7, 9, 10, 11
Klotz, Dr. John W. 139
Koster archipelago 22
Lamarck, Jean-Baptiste 18
Law of Conservation of Energy 32
Laws of Thermodynamics 32
Lead 59, 60, 67
Lecointre, Professor Guillaume 182, 183
Lenski experiment 21
Littorina saxatilis 22
lncRNA 26, 29
Loberg Lake 52, 54
Lomankus edgecombei 57, 58
Long
   Emma J. 59
Looy, Mark 144
Loxodonta
   africana 101
   cyclotis 101
Lucy 61
M'Farlane, Patrick 129
Macro-evolution 47, 48, 49, 50, 54

Magic....14, 34, 36, 37, 48, 51, 61, 69, 79, 84, 85, 96, 106, 115, 117
Mainstream evolutionary biologists 158
Malhan, Khyati 116
Mammals 19, 39
Mammoth 106
Mammuthus
   colunbi 101
   premogenius 101
Marx, Karl 189
Marxism 155, 157
Materialism 148, 190, 192, 195, 197
   overthrow of 190
Materialist 190
McKay, James 94
McKee, Edwin Dinwiddie 97
Megacheiran 57
Mega-evolution 137, 138
Metabolic pathways 33, 45, 56
Meyer, Stephen C. 11, 13, 14, 191
Micro-evolution 48, 138
Milankovitch cycles 109
Milky Way 115, 116, 117
Miller
   Hugh 129
Mishina, Tappei 42
Missing link 57, 61
Mitochondria 50
Modern humans 61, 62
Mohler, Dr. R. Albert, Jr 156
Moreton, Glenn 126
Morris, Henry Madison 138, 140, 143, 145, 147, 151, 152
Morris, John David 145
Mosaic
   Geology 128
   History 128
   law 130
Mosaical
   record 127

Index

statements 127
Mousterian 108
mRNA 26, 38, 42
Muav Limestone 97
Multicellular organisms 19, 20, 46, 47
Multicellularity 19
Muncaster, Ralph O. 152, 153
Murray, John 128
Mutation 10, 27, 36, 38, 39, 86
Myer, Stephen C. 125
Narlikar, Jayant 146
National Association of Biology Teachers 167, 172
Natural science 190, 196
Natural Selection 5, 20, 23, 24, 30, 33, 35, 36, 38, 56, 78, 80, 81, 142, 143, 144, 155, 157, 170, 179, 186, 187
Neanderthal 63, 102, 107, 108, 109
Neanderthal genes 102
Needless complexity 20
Needlessly complex 24
Neptunism 128
New Catastrophism 135
New genetic information 36, 121
New information 36
Newton, Isaac 127, 133
Noah's Ark 48, 87, 105
Nobel Laureates Initiative 178
Numbers, Ronald Leslie 131, 132
Objective moral standards 190
Occam, William of 43
Occam's Razor 44, 45, 85, 89, 123
O'Leary, Denyse 157
Ordovician 58
Orgel, Leslie 81
Palaeolithic
    Middle 107
Palaeoloxodon 101
    antiquus 101
    turkmenicus 100, 101
Palaeontology 196

Palley's Watch 33
Pan 64
Papastavrou, Nikolaos 81
Paranthropus 63
   boisei 63
   robustus 63
Parvati 118
Penn, Granville 127, 128
Petsko, Gregory A. 168
Pew Research Survey 5
Philosophy 127, 131, 137, 149, 150, 157, 169, 183, 196
   physical 127
Physics 36, 44, 163, 166, 190, 196
Pleistocene
   Middle 63
Pliocene 63
Pod Kopiste 50
Pod Mrcaru 50, 51
Podarcis
   melisellensis 50
   sicula 50
Political science 190
Politics 157, 190, 194, 196
Popper, DR. Karl 142
Powner, Professor Matthew 73
Price, George McCready 134, 136
Project Steve 187
Prokaryote 21, 46
Prolific waste 20
Proto-cell 77, 86
Psychology 190, 196
Pterodactyls 122
Puranas 118, 119
Purvis, Dr Graham 77
Pyritization 57, 58
Qiu, Lingqi 75
Qur'anic 'science' 126
Radiocarbon dating 90
Rana, Fazale 154

Index

Reardon, Patrick Henry 150
Red shift 116
Reilly, Amanda 93
Religious doctrine 169, 180
Religious dogma 9, 163, 175
Religious fundamentalist 126, 169
Retrotransposons 40
Retroviruses 39, 40
Richards, Jay Wesley 157
Rimmer, Harry 137
Rix, Hans-Walter 116
RNA 26, 29, 38, 39, 42, 46, 71, 78, 79, 80, 81, 82, 85, 86
    long non-coding 26
    messenger 26
    World hypothesis 80, 81
Ross, Hugh 148, 154
Rummo, Gregory J. 159
Saga, Carl 123, 124
Sagan, Carl Edward 148
Sahelanthropus tchadensis 64
Samper, Dr. Sofia C. 108
Satified with not knowing 18, 31
Scalidophora 66
Schaefer, Henry F. 153
Science education 171
Scientific consensus 6, 10, 14, 125, 126, 149, 162
Scientifically falsified, creationism 170
Scientifically useless, creationism 171
Scorpions 57, 66
Second Law of Thermodynamics 48
Selective environment 33, 45
Self-replicating molecules 122
Shakti 117, 118, 119
Shao, Professor Dr Yaping 103
Shiva 117, 118, 119
Shute, Evan Vere 138
Sieve of selection 122
Sinapis alba 30
Single-celled organisms 19, 20

Smith, Martin R. 59
Snelling, Dr. Andrew A. 94
Snelling, Dr. Andrew A. 93, 94, 95
Snoke, David W. 10
Social sciences 190, 192, 195, 197
Sociology 190
Special creation 133
Specification 34
Specified complexity 32, 35, 45
Spiders 57, 60, 65
Spriggina 67
Steppe bison 106
Straw man parody 47
Sub-optimal 14, 15, 20, 21
Sunderland, Luther D. 142
Supernatural designer 61
Supernatural entities 36, 51
Supreme Court 172
Syncytins 39
Tantras 118, 120
Tasmania 89, 90
Teach the controversy 167
Termes, Dr. Laura 106
The argument from ignorance Fallacy 13
The False Dichotomy Fallacy 14
The God of the Gaps Fallacy 13
The International Society for Science and Religion 186
The Kentucky Paleontological Society 176
The Lehigh University Department of Biological Sciences.177
The National Center for Science Education 172
The National Science Teachers Association 173
The Royal Astronomical Society of Canada, Ottawa Centre
 187
The Royal Society 188
Theology 44, 151, 186, 196
Theory in crisis 7, 11, 126
Theory of Evolution6, 7, 8, 11, 14, 23, 24, 45, 52, 54, 61, 66, 89, 121, 125, 126, 129, 136, 142, 154, 179, 183
Thermodynamics 32

Index

Thompson, Richard 156
Thymine 85
Tonto Group 96, 97
Tonto Platform 97
Tour, James M. 87, 125
Townsend, Reverend Luther Tracy 132
Tran, Quoc Phuong 78, 79
Transition 55, 64
Transitional form 55, 56, 57, 59, 61, 62, 63, 64
Transitional fossil 55, 61, 63, 64, 121
Transitional species 59, 61, 62
Transposons 15, 16, 17
Trilobite 58, 96, 97
Triplet code 85, 86
Type III secretion system 25
Uncus dzaugisi 65
Uniformitarian 143
Uniformitarianism 8
United Kingdom's Royal Society 185
United States National Academy of Sciences, Engineering,
    and Medicine 174
Universal probability bound 35
University of New South Wales 184
Upanishads 119, 120
U-Pb dating 59, 67
Uracil 85
Uranium 59, 60
US Constitution 125, 143
Vail, Newton Isaac 133
Varughese, T. V. 145
Vedas 118, 119, 120
Viperins 45, 46
Viruses 9, 39, 40, 46, 47
Vishnu 118
Volcanic tuffs 59, 67
Wallace, Alfred Russell 33, 126
Wedge
    Document 121, 189
    Projects, The 191

Strategy..........6, 7, 10, 11, 15, 125, 143, 149, 189, 191, 193
   Activities 197
   Five Year Goals...195, 196
   Five Year Strategic Plan...192
   Governing Goals 195
   Twenty Year Goals...195
Wegg-Prosser, F. R. 130
Wells, Jonathan 156
Whole genome duplication..36
Wilson, Dr. Clifford A 139
Wolbachia..42
Woolly rhinos..106
Wright, George Frederick 134
Xeroderma Pigmentosum..28
Yamnaya...111, 112, 113
Yang, Jie...59
Y-chromosome..112
YEC...23, 87, 94, 96, 117, 121
Yi, Ruiqin..78
Young Earth Creationists 23
Youti yuanshi...60
Zhang, Xiguang...59
Zhong, Professor Xuehua..16
Zircon 59, 60, 67
Zöckler, Professor Otto 131
Zygote..20
$\delta^{18}O$..109, 110

Other Books by Rosa Rubicondior

(Prices correct at time of publication. Check online for current details)

The Light of Reason Series:

The Light of Reason: And Other Atheist Writings.
Irreverent essays, thought-provoking articles and humorous items on atheism, religion, science, evolution, creationism and related issues.

(Hardcover|) ISBN-13: 979-8512173916	£13.75 (US $18.75)
(Paperback) ISBN-10: 1516906888, ISBN-13: 978-1516906888	£9.20 (US $12.75)
(Kindle) ASIN: B014N0IPVI	£5.50 (US $7.50)

The Light of Reason: Volume II – Atheism, Science and Evolution.
Thought-provoking essays on the conflict between fundamentalist religion and science, and exposing the anti-science, extremist political agenda of the modern creationist industry.

(Hardcover) ISBN-13: 979-8512191040	£13.75 (US $18.75)
(Paperback) ISBN-10: 1517105188, ISBN-13: 978-1517105181	£9.45 (US $11.75)
(Kindle) ASIN: B014N0IR16	£3.99 (US $5.99)

The Light of Reason: Volume III – Apologetics, Fallacies, and Other Frauds.
Thought-provoking essays and articles on religion and atheism, dealing with religious apologetics, fallacies, miracles and other frauds

(Hardcover) SBN-13: 979-8512526002	£13.90 (US $17.25)
(Paperback) ISBN-10: 151710761X, ISBN-13: 978-1517107611	£7.75 (US $10.75)
(Kindle) ASIN: B014N0IRE8	£3.50 (US $5.50)

The Light of Reason: Volume IV - The Silly Bible.
Exposing the absurdities, contradictions and historical inaccuracies in the Bible and advancing the case for atheism and against religion. This volume, the fourth in the Light of Reason series, deals with contradictions and absurdities in the Bible.

(Hardcover) ISBN-13: 979-8512539392	£13.75 (US $18.75)
(Paperback) ISBN-10: 1517108209, ISBN-13: 978-1517108205	£8.22 (US $10.20)
(Kindle) ASIN: B014N0IR8E	£3.99 (US $4.99)

The Light of Reason: And Other Atheist Writing. (all 4 volumes in one book)
Based on the Rosa Rubicondior science and Atheism blog, this is a collection of Atheist and science articles, some short, others lengthier, exploring the interface between religion and science and which have been published over some four years.

(Kindle only) ASIN: B013DYOK32	£6.34 (US $9.95)
(Paperback) ISBN-13: 978-1521146330	£24.00 (US $30.50)

The Failure of Creationism

Other books on science, Atheism and theology

An Unprejudiced Mind: Atheism, Science & Reason.
Essays on science and theology from a scientific atheist perspective, exploring particularly evolution versus creationism.

(Hardcover) ISBN-13: 979-8512554685	£13.35 (US $18.75)
(Paperback) ISBN-10: 1522925805, ISBN-13: 978-1522925804	£8.75 (US $11.75)
(Kindle) ASIN: B019UGXPM4	£3.99 (US $5.95)

Ten Reasons To Lose Faith: And Why You Are Better Off Without It.
Why faith is not only a fallacy and useless as a route to the truth but is actually harmful to society and to the individual. It systematically dismantles the standard religious apologetics and shows them to be bogus and deliberately constructed to mislead.

(Hardcover) ISBN-13: 979-8509108433	£18.90 (US $24.00)
(Paperback). ISBN-13:978-1530431953, ISBN–10: 1530431956	£12.60 (US $16.00)
(Kindle) ASIN: B01DGVO3JS	£6.90 (US $9.50)

What Makes You So Special? : From the Big Bang to You.
How did you come to be here, now? This book takes you from the Big Bang to the evolution of modern humans and the history of human cultures

(Hardcover) ISBN-13: 979-8509108433	£14.45 (US $18.40)
(Paperback) ISBN-13: 978-1546788294, ISBN-10: 1546788298	£10.00 (US $12.90)
(Kindle).ASIN: B071FTKXLZ	$5.69 (US $7.99)

Refuting Creationism: Why Creationism Fails In Both Its Science Its Theology
Creationism is not science and has no scientific validity. It' claims are untestable and free from supporting evidence and it makes no useful predictions. Arguments for it are invariably presupposition arguments from ignorant incredulity, god of the gaps and false dichotomy fallacies.

(Hardcover) ISBN: 979-8345634912	£14.13 (US $18.00)
(Paperback) ISBN: 979-8345104989	£9.81 (US $12.50)
(Kindle) ASIN B0DM2N14VW	£5.00 (US $6.50)

A History of Ireland: How Religion Poisoned Everything.
From the earliest beginnings to the Northern Ireland 'Troubles' and beyond. Religion has had a major role in spreading divisions and providing excuses for subjugation and repression. Only rarely has religion played a constructive role in the development of Irish culture and political life.

(Hardcover) ISBN-13: 979-8507235032	£15.75 (US $20.00)
(Paperback): ISBN-13: 978-1724988492	£9.50 (US $12.10)
(Kindle) ASIN: B07HHHRB34	£6.10 (US $7.25)

Other Books By Rosa Rubicondior

The Internet Handbooks series

The Internet Creationists' Handbook: A Joke for the Rest of Us.

A humorous look at creationist apologetics on the Internet, showing the fallacies and dishonest tactics creationists are using to try to recruit scientifically illiterate people into their political cult.

(Paperback),ISBN-13: 978-1721605149, ISBN-10: 1721605149   £5.78 (US $7.75)
(Kindle) ASIN: B07DZF75KD   £3.75 (US $5.00)

The Christian Apologists' Handbook: A Joke for the Rest of Us.

A humorous look at Christian apologetics on the Internet, showing the fallacies and dishonest tactics Christian fundamentalists are using to try to recruit scientifically and theologically illiterate people to their cults, often with political motives.

(Paperback) ISBN-13: 978-1721724727, ISBN-10: 1721724729   £6.25 (US $7.75)
(Kindle) ASIN: B07DYDVMW4   £3.75 (US $5.00)

The Muslim Apologists' Handbook: A Joke for the Rest of Us.

A humorous look at Muslim apologetics on the Internet, showing the fallacies and dishonest tactics Muslim fundamentalists are using to try to recruit scientifically and theologically illiterate people to their cuts, often with political motives.

(Paperback) ISBN-13: 978-1721756896, ISBN-10: 1721756892   £5.88 (US $7.75)
(Kindle) ASIN: B07DZF75KD $3.75 (US $5.00)

The Unintelligent Design Series

The Unintelligent Designer: Refuting the Intelligent Design Hoax

Showing why the superficial appearance of design in living things cannot be attributed to anything like an intelligent designer, as a counter to the politically motivated Intelligent Design movement.

(Hardcover) ISBN-13: 979-8513528463   £15.80 (US $20.00)
(Paperback) ISBN-10: 1723144215, ISBN-13: 978-1723144219   £11.20 (US $14.20)
(Kindle) ASIN B07G121BMK   £6.50 (US $7.50)

The Malevolent Designer: Why Nature's God is not Good

Showing why, so much of nature could not have been designed by an intelligent all-loving creator.
Illustrated by Catherine Hounslow-Webber

(Hardcover) ISBN-13: 979-8511295442   £16.70 (US $21.00)
(Paperback) SBN-13; 979-8670361729   £11.20 (US $14.15)
(Kindle) ASIN: B08L9S8F5F   £6.75 (US $8.00)

Publish under the name Bill Hounslow – Oxfordshire Childhood series.

In The Blink of an Eye: Growing Up in Rural Oxfordshire

A frank recollections of life as feral children in the small North Oxfordshire hamlet of Fawler during the 1950s and 60s, on the brink of major change as we approached the television age and the final stages in the domestication of children was about to begin.
Additional material by Patricia Broome

(Hardcover) ISBN-13: 979-8511967400	£14.90 (US $19.00)
(Paperback) ISBN-10: 1545350787, ISBN-13: 978-1545350782	£8.95 (US $11.40)
(Kindle) ASIN: B06ZY8JZ92	£6.95 (US $8.95)

In The Blink of an Eye: Growing Up in Rural Oxfordshire Illustrated Editions.

Illustrated by Catherine Webber-Hounslow

(Hardcover) ISBN-13; 979-8364521361	£16.90 (US $21.60)
(Paperback): ISBN-13:979-8364503862	£10.55 (US $13.50)
(Kindle) ASIN: B0BNCQG8CC	£7.50 (US $9.10)

A Goose for Christmas: Stories from an Oxfordshire Childhood

Slightly imaginative stories, based on real events and people, of childhood adventures in the North Oxfordshire hamlet of Fawler in the 1950s during the post-war austerity, before television, when the children had only what they could get from the woods and fields around them.
Illustrated by Catherine Webber-Hounslow

(Hardcover) ISBN-13: 979-8511907482	£14.90 (US $19.00)
(Paperback) ISBN-13: 978-1981708925, ISBN-10: 1981708928	£9.35 (US $11.90)
(Kindle) ASIN: B07GFJ85P8	£6.50 (US $8.25)

Printed in Great Britain
by Amazon